Painting the Eastern Shore

Painting the

Eastern Shore

A Guide to Chesapeake and Delaware Places and
How to Capture Them in Watercolors

James Drake Iams

The Johns Hopkins University Press

BALTIMORE AND LONDON

© 1999 The Johns Hopkins University Press
All rights reserved. Published 1999
Printed in the United States of America on acid-free paper
9 8 7 6 5 4 3 2 1

The Johns Hopkins University Press
2715 North Charles Street
Baltimore, Maryland 21218-4363
www.press.jhu.edu

Library of Congress Cataloging-in-Publication Data will be
found at the end of this book.
A catalog record for this book is available from the British Library.

ISBN 0-8018-6232-9

Contents

Introduction

The first watercolor I ever painted is still very vivid in my memory. During the winter of 1944, I needed to produce a painting for an art show in my elementary school. Like most kids that age, I procrastinated about going out to make a suitable sketch for the assignment. Finally, one Sunday afternoon, my mother took me by the hand and marched me up the street, in a freshly fallen snow, and down an alley to an old, abandoned blacksmith shop, and she sternly suggested I make a sketch from which I could paint my watercolor. Later that afternoon, from the sketch I had made, I painted a picture of the old blacksmith shop. The following week I won first prize for my effort. A photograph of me shaking hands with the judge, an art professor at the local state teachers' college, was in the local newspaper. I didn't paint another watercolor until my sophomore year at that same teachers' college.

On graduation from college, I accepted a position teaching art in a high school in the Baltimore County public school system. The city of Baltimore, the Patapsco River, the harbor, and the Chesapeake Bay stirred my creative juices, and I fell in love with the area.

The Chesapeake Bay, with its inlets and coves and tributaries, is one of the premier sailing areas in the United States. For many—and surely for anyone as fascinated by boats as I am—this makes the region even

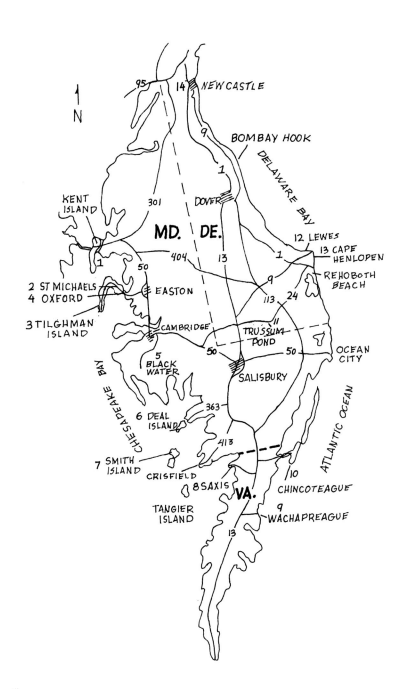

more appealing. During the late spring, summer, and early fall, up to Thanksgiving, you will see sailing craft and motor launches virtually everywhere, cruising the ever-changing waters of the Bay. And in all seasons, commercial vessels—tugs, barges, tankers, container ships, and freighters—ply the waterways.

Across the Chesapeake Bay from Annapolis is the *Eastern Shore*. It is a generally flat land, dotted with farms and villages, with water of some sort virtually everywhere you turn. In addition to the Chesapeake Bay itself, there are streams and tidal rivers, inlets and little bays, and acres and acres of marshes. And many, many marinas.

The Eastern Shore is the eastern shore of the Chesapeake Bay. Although the term, strictly speaking, refers solely to those counties of Maryland and Virginia that lie to the east of the Bay, there are those who consider the Eastern Shore to be essentially synonymous with the Delmarva Peninsula. *Delmarva,* of course, stands for Delaware, Maryland, and Virginia. The peninsula includes all of the state of Delaware, nine counties of Maryland, and two of Virginia. From Delaware Bay in the north, it extends south to Cape Charles at the mouth of the Chesapeake Bay. It is bounded on the west by the Chesapeake Bay and on the east by the Atlantic Ocean. Delmarva is a haven for bird watchers (being on the Atlantic flyway) and also for waterfowl hunters. More importantly, it is a painter's paradise. Artists who explore the peninsula will discover richly picturesque areas with eminently paintable scenes in every hamlet, marina, marsh, and vista.

One of the appeals of the area is that, compared to the megalopolis stretching from Washington, D.C., to Boston, it is remarkably rural and underpopulated. Until a generation ago, visitors to Delmarva drove down into the peninsula from the north or they came by ferry across the Bay. Since people did not pass through the area on their way to somewhere else, the natives had Delmarva pretty much to themselves. Even since the advent of a bridge across the Bay and a bridge-tunnel connecting the southern tip of Delmarva to Norfolk, Virginia, the peninsula still seems a bit remote, and parts of it seem truly to have been bypassed by the twentieth century. The towns are small. Even the cities are small. Except for the major thoroughfares, the traffic is relatively light. Once outside of town, you are in the country—until you come to the next village or crossroad. The countryside, gently rolling in the north and flattening as you go south, alternates between farms and wood lots. Marshes dominate some of the southern counties.

Because the area is so appealing and picturesque, tourism has become a burgeoning industry. The Eastern Shore has indeed been discovered by an ever-growing number of urbanites. As a consequence, there is no dearth of restaurants, motels, B&Bs, campgrounds, and the like, and, as you would expect, these facilities range from mom-and-pop simplicity to the luxurious.

As off the beaten track as it is, the Eastern Shore is easily reached. It is scarcely more than an hour's drive from Washington, Baltimore, or Philadelphia. It is only a little more than that from Richmond, from eastern Pennsylvania, or from southern New Jersey. It is scarcely a half-day's drive from New York.

IN THE PROCESS of introducing you to the fundamentals of watercolor painting, I will lead you up, down, and around—back and forth across the Delmarva Peninsula. I will take you to interesting places to sketch and paint, many of them my favorite haunts. On the way, at each stop, I will paint a watercolor, demonstrating the many aspects of transparent watercolor and stressing one particular technique. I will discuss drawing, composition, value, color, and control of the medium and will suggest subjects to stimulate your creativity and heighten your response to what is there. Touring historic towns and learning something of their backgrounds will fuel your enthusiasm to paint the local scene. And there is always the chance of encountering an Eastern Shore waterman, in his fertilizer hat and rubber boots, willing to answer a question or two, giving you a glimpse into life on the water.

BEFORE SETTING OUT on our trip, I want to discuss the equipment you will need. Many students carry and drag beach chairs, card tables, umbrellas, satchels filled with drawing boards, pads of paper, rolls of paper towels, and, of course, paints, a palette, and a bundle of brushes. Much of this equipment is useful, but in the field you need to keep things compact and easy to carry.

My field equipment, when I began painting, included a small folding metal stool, and I placed my work on the ground. This meant bending over for long periods, which was very hard on my back, and my legs often went to sleep. Now I carry a paint box about $16'' \times 20''$, with a T-nut fastener in the bottom. (A T-nut fastener is a metal collar designed to be inserted through a thin piece of wood. It has little teeth to keep it from turning and is threaded on the inside to accept a threaded bolt. Hardware stores carry them, usually in several sizes.) The T-nut permits me to attach my paint box to a camera tripod. In the lid of the box, I can carry a $15'' \times 20''$ watercolor block. The bottom of the box is divided into compartments to hold brushes, paints, a water bottle, a paint cloth, and the sundry materials needed to paint a painting. My box was made for me by a fellow artist, but one can use any paint box, even an attaché case reinforced on the bottom with quarter-inch plywood. Insert a T-nut in the center of the plywood panel, and you are all set. For convenience in carrying your rig, you can attach your tripod to the box with a couple of straps. I used leather dog collars for mine. Punch holes in the collars, and drill holes in the box. Using short bolts with lock nuts, fasten the straps down. (See diagram.) This rig is so convenient to take with me when I travel that I refer to my box as my *carry-on luggage*. I usually carry a folding stool, but I prefer to stand when I paint. When I get tired, which often happens, I sit a spell and then continue.

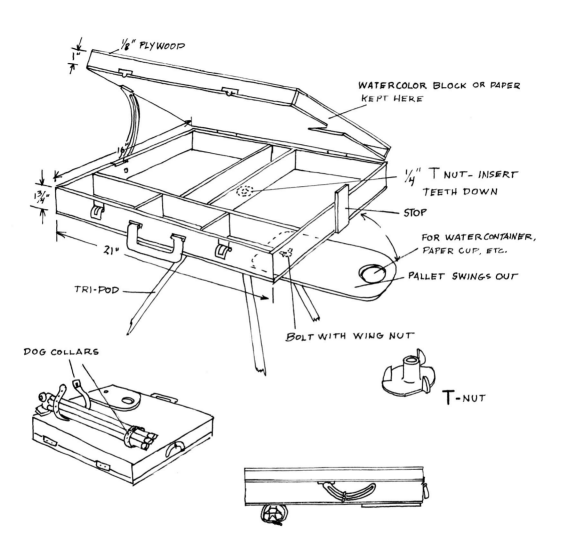

1/8" PLYWOOD

1"

16"

13/4"

21"

TRI-POD

WATERCOLOR BLOCK OR PAPER KEPT HERE

1/4" T NUT- INSERT TEETH DOWN

STOP

FOR WATER CONTAINER, PAPER CUP, ETC.

PALLET SWINGS OUT

BOLT WITH WING NUT

T-NUT

DOG COLLARS

The tripod-and-box setup is not terribly steady. It tends to move up and down or wiggle a little when pressure is applied, and although I am used to it, some find this bothersome. On the other hand, it is so easy to paint outdoors with a rig like this—to go plein-air painting, as the French would say. Suntan lotion, a broadbrim hat, occasionally some bug repellent, and a positive attitude are all very important, not to say essential.

Now we are ready to sketch and paint. Let's go.

Painting the Eastern Shore

CHAPTER ONE

Kent Narrows, Maryland : Drawing

Drawing and painting the Chesapeake workboat.
What to look for. Understanding the different
objects found on the boats.

et's begin our expedition on the Western Shore and approach our destination by driving east on U.S. Route 50 across the Chesapeake Bay
Bridge, from the direction of Washington, Baltimore, or Annapolis. The
eastern end of the bridge span brings you onto Kent Island. You are now
on the Eastern Shore, as a welcoming sign will tell you. Continuing on a
few more miles, crossing the flat, narrow island, you will come to Kent
Narrows, where the highway goes over a high, arching bridge. As you approach the bridge, watch for Exit 41, a road leading off to the right
marked *Kent Narrows West.* This will take you to a workboat basin where
watermen tie up their craft. These workboats are worth study and several sketches.

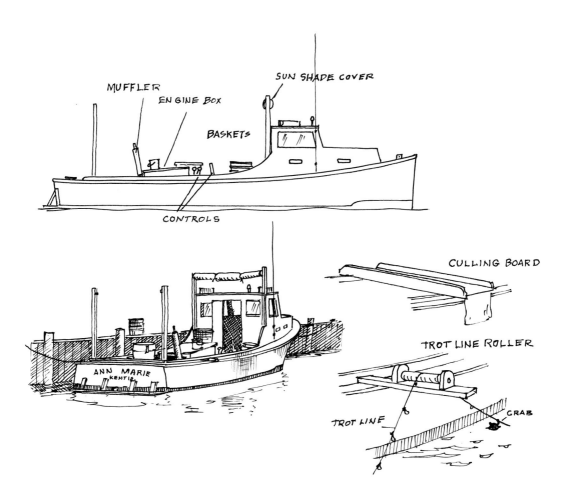

MUFFLER

ENGINE BOX

SUN SHADE COVER

BASKETS

CONTROLS

CULLING BOARD

ANN MARIE
KENT IS.

TROT LINE ROLLER

TROT LINE

CRAB

Most of these workboats are in the neighborhood of thirty-two feet in length. This length keeps the boats from hobby-horsing on the choppy waters of the Chesapeake Bay. Many of the newer boats are constructed of fiberglass, but most are built of wood. The cuddy cabin is sufficient for storing gear, supplies, and a radio phone and for keeping the skipper and his helper out of the inclement weather that blows up quickly on the Bay. Wooden baskets stacked haphazardly on the deck are used to store the day's catch. A bucket, cooler, bait box, and trash container are all part of the scene. In the summer, most of the boats will be equipped for trotlining, one of the methods of catching the Bay's famous blue crabs. Briefly, trotlining consists of laying a stout line, usually hundreds of yards long and baited at about six-foot intervals, along the shallow bottom of the Bay. An anchor and a small buoy are attached to each end. The workboat cruises slowly down the line, having threaded it over a roller. This roller is on the end of a *prop stick,* which extends out from the starboard (right) gunwale of the boat, a few feet above the water. As the boat moves, it continually lifts a moving portion of the line up from the bottom and over the roller; with it, tenaciously holding onto the bait, will be crabs. On boats equipped for trotlining, the engine controls are on the starboard side of the boat. The tiller, a vertical handle or lever for steering the boat, is about halfway back in the cockpit, next to the clutch and throttle. Look for their red and green knobs. The waterman stands beside them,

Plate 1. Workboat Basin, Kent Narrows, *10" × 14"*

controls the motor, steers the boat, and works the trotline using his dip net. He must net each crab before it breaks the water, or the crab will most likely drop off and elude capture.

Most boats have a canvas cover over the aft deck, supported by four poles—one at each corner of the deck. If there is no cover on the boat, more than likely the poles are still there, as if marking the corners of the deck area. Summers on the Chesapeake Bay can be intense, and the shade created by these covers is very welcome.

Study the boats carefully. The drawings on these pages will point out many of the details you will need to know in order to render these boats accurately. (See also color plate 1.)

In addition to trotlines for crabs, several other rigs are used, depending on what is to be caught and how. Another distinctive rig, for example, is used for clamming. Different rigs are used when patent tonging or hand tonging for oysters. In the winter, in oyster season, these workboats will have a culling board laid between the gunwales, across the deck. The culling board is aptly named, for it is there that the watermen sort, or cull, their oyster catch, separating live and legal-sized oysters from dead and small ones and swiping the discards overboard. The freeboard, or side of the boat, under the end of the culling board is invariably stained from all the muck pushed off into the water. By the end of the winter, the boats all look a bit used.

Hand tonging consists of catching oysters by using long, scissors-like tongs, usually from a small workboat. Two long wooden poles, attached together by a pivot a few feet from the bottom and with a toothed metal basket on the ends, are dropped straight down as the waterman stands precariously on the gunwale of the boat. In a movement very much like using a posthole digger, he thrusts the basket onto the bay floor and pulls the poles, or *shafts,* together and then apart, gathering up to perhaps a third of a bushel of oysters in the basket. Then, hand over hand, he draws up his harvest and dumps the load onto the culling board. This takes considerable strength. One man tongs and a second culls the catch. The shafts vary in length from fourteen to sometimes more than twenty feet, and the depth of the water determines which length to use. (See the sketch.)

A patent tonging rig consists of a much larger iron basket, which, instead of being attached to shafts, is suspended from a cable. The basket is dropped to the bottom from a boom mounted amidship and is hauled up by power. *Patent,* in nautical usage, is a term for a new (not necessarily patented) piece of equipment that replaces an old standby. Color plate 7 illustrates a patent tonging rig.

CHAPTER TWO

St. Michaels, Maryland : Perspective

Creating the illusion of the third dimension.

I want to take you to the popular town of St. Michaels and use the visit there to study perspective. From the Bay Bridge, drive east on U.S. 50 toward Easton. Just as you approach Easton, you will see an overhead sign for St. Michaels, directing you to bear right onto Maryland 322 (Easton Parkway). After about a mile and a half, turn right onto Maryland 33. This will lead, in about ten miles, to the attractive, low-key town of St. Michaels.

A motel, a restaurant, some gas stations, and other roadside attractions—along with a reduced speed limit—herald your approach to this tourist-oriented community. You will be on Talbot Street, St. Michaels' main street. You will notice scores of shops, several restaurants, churches, and well-kept houses. There is a lot to explore, but not yet. Continue along Talbot Street, watch for Mill Street on your right, and follow the signs to the Chesapeake Bay Maritime Museum parking area. The Maritime Museum itself should probably be your first visit. The Hooper Strait Lighthouse dominates the grounds, and the museum's fleet of Chesapeake sailing craft and workboats, along with their permanent and changing exhibits, dramatize the history and lore of the region. The museum collection provides a wonderful opportunity, incidentally, to examine workboats up close, to take an unhurried look at their fittings, rigging, and other details that are sometimes hard to see when you view a workboat from a distance.

After your visit to the museum, stroll along the brick walk, toward town, next to the harbor. The Crab Claw Restaurant will be on your left, and a large figurehead under the protecting balcony of a museum building will be on your right. Continue past the tied-up workboats and across a little bridge. Bed-and-breakfast options will be on either side. You are now on Cherry Street. Turn left onto Locust Street and proceed to Carpenter Street. To your left, down at the harbor's edge, is the Higgins Boatyard. In the right foreground is an attractive house. Let's stop here, make a sketch and a watercolor painting of this house, and use it to explore the important subject of perspective.

THE SURFACE of a painting is two dimensional, and any lines drawn on the surface have only length and width. A two-dimensional painting or design may be successful, but in representational painting, particularly landscape painting, perspective is essential, for it is perspective that creates the illusion of a third dimension on a two-dimensional surface. The ability to portray perspective successfully is acquired only through study and solid understanding.

There are several ways in which the illusion is achieved. One of the ba-

Figure 2-1

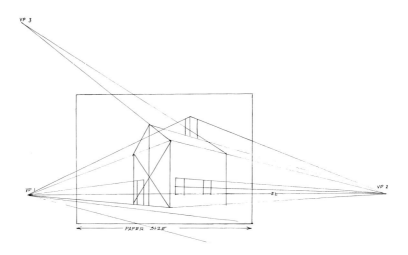

sic techniques is to use *linear perspective.* You have noticed that the farther away things are, the smaller they appear to be. Logic tells you that, if they recede far enough into the distance, they will disappear entirely. The point at which they disappear is called the *vanishing point.* If you look at a house, which is composed of flat planes with vertical and horizontal edges, you will notice that, although the verticals look vertical, the horizontal lines—the foundation lines, the eaves, the tops and bottoms of doors and windows, and so forth—appear to slant.

Figure 2-1 demonstrates *three-point perspective.* It shows why the horizontal lines appear to slant. You first establish an eye level, three vanishing points, and lines leading to them. One vanishing point will be off the paper to the right, another off to the left. And, in this example, the third one is somewhere off toward Mars. Despite my example, and as effective as it is, I don't want to stress this method of creating the illusion of a third dimension because I don't want you to rely on rulers or other means of establishing these lines. A ruled line can be very sterile and uninteresting. I prefer another method.

The secret to correct perspective is establishing correct proportions between the various objects in the composition—the size or height of a telephone pole in relation to the house next to it, for example, or the size of the front of the house in relation to the back of the house. Or the height of fences in relation to the animals behind them, or the relation between people and the objects around them. Placing people in your painting quickly establishes the scale of everything else in the picture. The first thing, then, in beginning a painting is to find the object you intend to use as the reference point—the object to which all other objects in the painting relate.

Here is a simple, helpful exercise. Use a pencil to assist you in seeing relative sizes and shapes. In figure 2-2, you can see that by holding your pencil horizontally at eye level you can more easily determine the slant of lines. The pitch of the roof on the house slopes sharply down to the left to the closest corner of the house. The angle of the slope, thanks to this pencil guide, is more easily seen. By holding the pencil vertically, you can

Figure 2-2

Figure 2-3

easily see the differences in height or proportion of the house and the telephone pole. Your pencil becomes a kind of ruler by which you "measure" one height against another. Once you establish the height of the house in your drawing, all other items in the composition will fall into place. I use this proportional method of perspective all the time as I sketch. Overlapping of objects (closer ones blocking out things behind them, for example) and intensity of color also affect our sense of the third dimension. I will be dealing with these later.

The greatest single challenge that faces beginning painters is drawing—blocking out your composition on your paper. To ease this process, establish the size of one object and relate all other items to it. This sounds too simple to be important, but it is.

In the painting of Carpenter Street (color plate 2), the side of the house closest to me runs almost parallel to the bottom of the paper. If I had used linear perspective, the vanishing point for the siding on the

Plate 2. Carpenter Street, *15" × 22"*

house would lie about a mile away on the right. There is very little cant to the lines of the clapboards. The left side of the house is another story. The third dimension was determined by holding my pencil vertically and relating the boat, on chocks, to the front roof line. The trees, windows, and poles were similarly related one to the other.

ST. MICHAELS offers endless painting opportunities. As you wander down Talbot Street, turn onto East Mulberry and then right into St. Mary's Square. It will delight you. A block further on, East Chew Avenue leads to the workboat basin. There you get a panoramic view of the harbor, an array of boats, and houses overlooking the water. There are as many scenes to sketch and paint as your time permits. And more.

CHAPTER THREE

Tilghman Island, Maryland: Skipjacks

*Sketching and painting skipjacks. Studying standing
and running rigging. The parts of a skipjack.*

Tilghman Island is about twelve miles beyond St. Michaels on
Maryland 33. The land is flat, with farms and wood lots on either
side of the road. Eventually you will head down a narrow peninsula, with
water intermittently visible on both sides—the Chesapeake Bay on your
right and Harris Creek (which leads into the Choptank River) on your
left. As you approach Tilghman, you will see the masts of boats tied up
in the gut called *Knapps Narrows,* and, as you get closer, you will see the
drawbridge. This overhead-counterweight drawbridge is a wonder. It is a
"heel trunnion rolling lift bridge [quoting the *Baltimore Sun*] with the
counterweight above the roadway, built in 1934." The only one in the

state, it looks like nothing else, but it has seen its day and is being replaced. Preservationists, island residents, and state officials have agreed that its replacement, being build right next to it, will retain the old bridge's characteristic towering look. When the new bridge opens, this beautiful old relic will be dismantled, moved, and reconstructed on the grounds of the Chesapeake Maritime Museum in St. Michaels.

But back to our journey. Once you have crossed over one of the busiest drawbridges in the country, you are on Tilghman Island, one of my favorite haunts.

Knapps Narrows is a very busy waterway between the Chesapeake Bay and the Choptank River. Workboats and pleasure craft move frequently through the narrows, blowing their horns for the bridge, which seems to open every few minutes. Several buyboats are tied up along this narrow channel, along with sailboats, motor launches, and a variety of workboats. A packing company stands near the bridge, ready to buy and process the catch of the day from the local watermen.

Beyond the bridge, about a quarter-mile on the left, is Dogwood Harbor, where more working boats are tied up. I have seen as many as seven skipjacks in this harbor at one time. The smaller power workboats move in and out with their loads of crabs, clams, or oysters, depending on the time of year. Dogwood Harbor is not the neatest or cleanest place. Eastern Shore watermen tend to clutter up the waterfront with various sundry items and leftover boat parts.

Don't set up to paint at an empty slip. More than likely, once you have started your painting, a waterman will enter the cove and back his boat into the empty slip you have selected, cutting off your view. This has happened to me several times. The watermen, though, are very pleasant and are generally tolerant of artists.

SKIPJACKS are the most celebrated sailboats on the Chesapeake Bay. Numbering perhaps five hundred at the turn of the twentieth century, there now are as few as twelve skipjacks dredging the oyster beds of the Bay and its tributaries—the last commercial fleet under sail in the country. The skipjack is a vee-bottom, centerboard sailboat, commonly thirty-five to sixty feet in length, with a single, raking mast. Skipjacks were developed in the Chesapeake Bay in the 1880s for oyster dredging and general fishing. Simple in design, they could be constructed by a good general carpenter (as distinct from a shipwright), were relatively inexpensive to build, and required but a small crew. Their mainsail is huge, with the boom extending well beyond the stern of the boat. This large sail permits skipjacks to pull their heavy dredges across the bottom steadily, even in a light breeze.

Current regulations require that oyster dredging on the Bay be done Monday and Tuesday under power and Wednesday, Thursday, and Friday under sail. Oystermen work five days a week. Skipjacks have no auxiliary engines, so power is provided by yawls, or push boats, that hang on davits across the stern when not in use and are lowered when power is needed. In operation, the push boat is nuzzled into a V-shaped wooden chock on the stern of the skipjack, its motor handily furnishing the needed power.

Built of wood and iron, these graceful boats, none of them very young, suffer from general wear and tear through the years, not to mention the constant beating from the weather and salt water. During the summer most of them get a fresh coat of paint and a general overhaul in preparation for the fall dredging. Before dredging begins, however, while they are all in their fresh splendor, working skipjacks race annually at Deal Island on Labor Day and off Sandy Point State Park (at the western end of the Chesapeake Bay Bridge) on the last weekend of October. These are not painting opportunities, specifically, but they are great fun to watch.

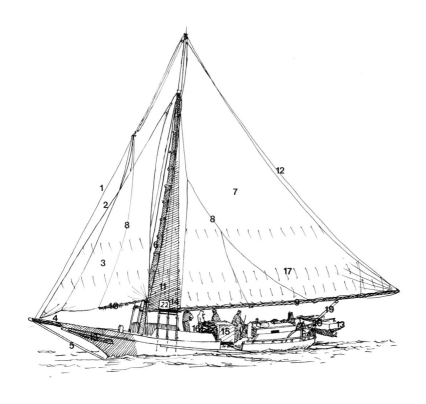

Figure 3-1. Skipjack:
1, forestay; 2, jibstay;
3, jib; 4, bowsprit;
5, bobstay; 6, mast;
7, mainsail; 8, lazy Jack;
9, boom; 10, jib boom
(mutton leg); 11, shrouds;
12, topping lift; 13, push
boat; 14, dredge number;
15, engine box; 16, dredge
winch; 17, reefing points;
18, trail board; 19, sheet;
20, davit.

DRAWING THE SKIPJACK can prove challenging. The curve of the boat and its sheer, the rake of the mast, the long boom, and other details require close observation and study. It is essential that you understand how the boat works—what purpose each part or fitting serves. There is nothing extraneous on the boat; everything is there for a reason. I have drawn a skipjack and named its essential parts so you may better understand what you are seeing. I have not, however, illustrated the halyards. The halyards (running rigging) are the lines (ropes) used to hoist and lower the sails. There is a jib halyard and a main halyard, both usually running up the mast and cleated off at the base, near the deck. If, when you are sketching, you're in doubt as to what you are looking at, get up

and walk over for a better look, but don't go on board unless you are invited by the skipper.

These are beautiful boats, with their clipperlike bowsprits, their trail boards, their varnished wooden masts and booms, with painted white mast tops and boom ends. When you see these skipjacks in Dogwood Harbor, their mainsails are furled and tied to the boom with short lines, or stops. Often the jib lies atop the bowsprit, also tied down. The dredges rest on deck next to the power winch used to haul them up. When dredging, the cables to which the dredges are attached are played out on either side of the boat over metal rollers, about midship, just above deck level. There is usually obvious wear at the stern end of the roller. This is caused by the cable rubbing and cutting into the timber as the skipjack moves steadily forward while the dredges are being pulled in. Note, too, the inevitable rust and mud stains on the side of the boat beneath the roller.

A painting begun in Dogwood Harbor (color plate 3) offers a bow-on view of a skipjack, which was rafted up to a buyboat, and on the right, in the background, are several more skipjacks. The bowsprit comes right toward the viewer, almost breaking the picture plane. A painting, after all, is two-dimensional. The *picture plane* is, essentially, the surface of a painting. With various perspective devices, the relative placement of objects, and the use of color, the painter creates the illusion of a third dimension. In this instance, the unusual perspective gives the painting a more-than-usual appearance of depth and almost exaggerates the interruption of the picture plane. Keeping the background light tends to make it recede, adding to this illusion, while the reflections from the boats are strong and detailed. The reflections aid in placing the skipjacks in, as distinct from on, the water. (I discuss and demonstrate reflections in chapter 12.)

Dogwood Harbor is a large painting (22″ × 30″). I actually painted it in my studio, using sketches and a smaller painting done on Tilghman Island, along with some photographs taken at the same time. I often do

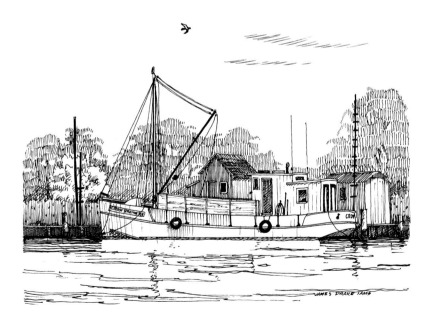

Figure 3-2. The Buyboat

this: paint a larger version of a small painting, especially when I feel the subject would be more successfully portrayed in a larger format. Specific items like ropes and chains and even such things as cast shadows can be handled in more detail in the larger painting. And, to be frank, this procedure also gives me a chance to study the scene with a bit more care and to make a correction or two.

As I introduced you to Tilghman Island, I mentioned the boats tied up in Knapps Narrows, and among these were *buyboats*. This actually is an anachronism. I use the term to mean somewhat larger motor craft than the usual workboat that is used for trotlining for crabs or tonging for oysters, but buyboats are things of the past. In the days when the dredge boats stayed out for days at a time, and sometimes weeks, buyboats intercepted them to take off their catch and get it promptly to market. They were large enough to stow the catches of a number of skipjacks (and the catches were much larger in those days than they are now), and they made their rounds daily, sometimes bringing supplies to the skipjacks as they hauled the bounty off to the packing houses. Now the skipjacks come home every evening and deliver their catch either directly to the wholesaler or to his truck on the dock. But the buyboats, now put to other uses, remain. I'm intrigued by them and have illustrated one.

CHAPTER FOUR

Oxford, Maryland : Value

*Studying value, dark and light, in a composition. Shadows and
how they describe form. Transparency and its application.*

*O*xford is one of the oldest settlements in Maryland and, indeed,
was the first town on Maryland's Eastern Shore. Settled in the
1660s, Oxford prospered because of its location on the Tred Avon River,
with its deep-water anchorage that could accommodate the largest
ocean-going vessels of the day and its broad waterfront area where
wharves and warehouses could be built. In 1694, the General Assembly
named Oxford and Ann Arundell (now Annapolis) the two sole ports of
entry for the entire Maryland province. Oxford thrived. By the end of the
eighteenth century, the pattern of agriculture was changing, however,
and tobacco slowly giving way to more profitable grain. Oxford, largely

dependent on tobacco merchants, began to decline. Concurrently, Baltimore, with its accessibility to the inland market, was becoming a major port. Eventually, oystering, fishing, and clamming, as well as the introduction of the railroad in the mid–nineteenth century, brought life back to Oxford.

Nothing in the village, however, suggests that Oxford was more than a century old before the American Revolution; all of the really old houses have disappeared. Today Oxford is a neat, spotlessly clean town where tourists stroll the brick sidewalks along beautiful tree-lined streets, where each house along Morris Street is whiter and better kept than its neighbor, and where each little side street invites exploration. There are restaurants and gift shops, a crescent beach, and a quiet park overlooking the river. There are five flourishing boatyards and three marinas.

Oxford is but a short drive from Tilghman Island. Retrace your drive up the peninsula on Route 33, back through St. Michaels. A couple of miles farther, and a sign on the right will indicate the turn for the Bellevue-Oxford Ferry. The blacktop road winds its way to the small community of Royal Oak, where you will make a right turn, following the signs to Bellevue. The road will meander, but within a few miles it will end at a pier overlooking the Tred Avon River, considered by many sailors to be the most attractive river on the Eastern Shore. The water tower on the opposite shore, standing tall at the head of Town Creek, proclaims *Oxford.* Cars often must wait for the ferry to arrive from the other side, but the wait is never long. The ferry slip is at the mouth of a basin usually filled with workboats, so there is plenty to look at while you wait. This is a pleasant and picturesque scene. Often bicyclists will also be waiting to sandwich themselves in among the automobiles crossing on the ferry. The ride across the river takes about ten minutes, which is not as long as many would like, since there is scarcely time to see all the sail and motor boats on the river, to watch Bellevue slip away behind, and to appreciate Oxford, which seems to materialize all too quickly. On your left, as you approach the ferry slip, is the entrance to Town Creek. On your right is the Tred Avon Yacht Club. Upon leaving the ferry, you will be facing the imposing Robert Morris Inn, overlooking the water at the north end of Morris Street.

The other way to Oxford is, of course, by land. In that case, you take Maryland 333 from Easton. After about a ten-mile drive, you enter the town by skirting the end of Town Creek, and then go north on Morris Street. If you take Morris Street about a mile to the end, you will be at the ferry slip.

OXFORD is a nice town to walk or drive around in, but for now, we'll head for Cutts & Case Boatyard, which is where we will set up our paint box and paint our watercolor. To get there from the ferry, drive a few blocks on Morris Street and then take a left at Tilghman Street. After about two blocks the boatyard will be on your right. From the other direction, Tilghman Street will be on your right off Morris Street, not far past the park.

Once at Cutts & Case, look for a place to park. Space is often available on the right, near the small building next to the drive. By and large, you are safe parking where there are already a few cars, but it is important not to block the operation of the yard.

Cutts & Case is a busy working yard, one of the very few wood repair and wood construction yards on the East Coast. The numerous boats up on chocks, in the water, and under cover in the sheds will testify to this. A wooden boat under construction can usually be found in the shed at the head of the marine railway. The odor of sawdust and the smell of cedar, pine, mahogany, varnish, and paint give the yard a distinctive atmosphere all its own. Boats under repair, freshly painted spars lying on well-worn sawhorses, and the sound of a band saw running in the workshop vie for your attention.

But first things first. Introduce yourself to one of the workmen and ask to speak to Ed Cutts, the owner of the yard. Wherever you go to paint, always introduce yourself to the owner of the property. At the very least, it is the courteous thing to do, and the owners appreciate the thoughtfulness. You don't want to be an unwelcome trespasser.

At Cutts & Case, Ed welcomes artists to paint in and around his yard and, if he is not too busy, will give you a tour and relate the history of the yard. The tour is informative and interesting. The yard was established in the 1920s by Ralph Wiley and bore his name. He was a marine architect and the builder of some of the finest sailing craft on the Bay. He also knew how to sail them and win races. You can still see many of his double-ended sailboats out on the piers and in the bright red shed at the rear of the workshop. If you like boats and water as much as I do, you will love this boatyard. Traditional wood boats, of all kinds, stir my creative juices, and I can't wait to get started on a watercolor painting.

Before you begin to sketch and paint, explore the whole yard. Investigate every shed, but, as I have said before, be sure not to interrupt or interfere with any of the work being done. Your wanderings will help you pick a location in which to set up and paint.

I have set up my watercolor equipment in several locations in the boatyard, and for this demonstration I selected the pier between the marine railway and the house. From this location I can paint the boat on the railway and include the near side of the boat shed.

My aim in this painting is to concentrate on *value*—the light and dark pattern in the composition—and to stress the importance of the relationship between light and dark. Value can be thought of as the relative degrees of lightness and darkness as measured by the amount of light reflected from objects. More simply, it is the pattern of these tones—a pattern that is as important to the finished painting as drawing is, or even sometimes as important as color. Another term closely related to value is *chiaroscuro,* from the Italian words for *clear,* or light, and *obscure,* or dark. This term is sometimes used to describe the treatment of the

white and black, or light and dark, parts in a pictorial work of art and the strong contrast between objects.

When you paint outdoors, the natural sunlight will dictate where the darks and cast shadows appear. Record them as you see them, right at the beginning, by sketching the scene, indicating the dark and light patterns, because as the day progresses the shadows will change. Those areas that appear to be lost in shadow are just as important as the areas that stand out in sunlight. In color plate 4 (painted on a 14" × 20" block of Winsor & Newton 140-pound hot press paper), the white hull of the boat *Ariel* is in high contrast with the red-orange building and the dark green trees on the right. The deep shadows under the boat tie the darks together and emphasize the hull even more.

Here are some tips to help you with value. One is to view the scene through a piece of colored plastic or glass; the black-and-white pattern shows clearly. This is a trick or crutch often used by amateurs, and it helps, but I prefer another method: I squint. Squinting tends to eliminate most of the middle tones, and the dominant light and dark patterns will stand out dramatically. In other words, squinting your eyes will help you to see the patterns or areas of darks and lights.

In addition to creating interesting patterns, shadows perform another valuable service. They help describe the surface shapes of objects. In our example the cast shadow under the eaves, on the left end of the shed, indicates the length of the roof overhang. The shadow under the slanted tin roof to the left of the boat also helps describe the size of that overhang.

Also note that the shadows are transparent. If shadows are not kept transparent, they will look like cutout pieces of colored paper. One way to keep them transparent is to paint them with a wash of tinted color, such as a thin glaze of a gray-blue. It is essential that you make sure the underpainting is bone dry before you apply a glaze. To deepen the shadow, you can apply two or more layers of thin glaze, being sure each time that the underpainting is perfectly dry.

In this painting, both the cast shadows of the trees on the right side of the white hull and the shadow cast by the boat itself on the side of the shed were painted with a gray-blue transparent glaze. Painting outside, as I was, my paint was drying rather quickly, so I didn't have to wait very long for the areas to become dry enough to allow application of the glazes.

I usually work from the light passages to the dark areas in my paintings. You can always darken an area in a painting, but making a dark area lighter presents a problem. Whatever else, opaque white is not the answer. I like a true aquarelle watercolor.

After sketching the scene on my paper, I began by painting the sky. This day was sunny and bright, so a wash of light cerulean blue with some high, puffy clouds captured the mood of the morning. With such a light sky, the background trees can be painted over the sky once it is dry. Using a half-inch flat brush, I mixed cadmium red medium with a

touch—just a touch—of cadmium yellow medium and painted the sunny side of the work shed. Later I used the same mix, but added a mixture of sepia and cobalt blue, for the shadowed side of the building. In this instance I did not use a wash or glaze, but rather added darker pigments to my base color.

Color is such a personal thing. No two artists, even when painting the same scene, will use the same palette. In chapter 7 I deal with handling color, but here I simply want to indicate where I began the painting and my choices of colors. In any painting of yours, you will make your own, uniquely personal decisions.

I painted the bright leaves of the tree on the right and then added the middle gray-green, followed by the dark leaves. The tree trunk was the last thing painted. (There is more about trees, also, later in the book.) The foreground grass can be a blister to paint. I take pains to be patient and paint carefully, since this is just as important as the rest of the painting. I studied the pier and particularly observed the shadows and the pattern the shadows make on the pier. While most of the detail under the boat was left purposely obscure, I nevertheless paid attention to the braces and underpinnings so as to keep things believable. The doorway into the shed is dark, and you will notice that I created depth by showing a window on the far side of the shed and letting the light from it and the open door suggest some boards leaning against the wall inside.

I was well into my painting when the workman appeared. I did a quick sketch of him and, once back in my studio, using gouache paint, added him to the scene. A human figure often adds a nice touch and also helps create a sense of scale.

I have been to the Cutts & Case yard many times, and I never tire of it. I'm confident that you will enjoy the same experience. Subject matter abounds in a setting like this, and it offers the artist unlimited opportunities for great watercolors. If you visit here once, I predict that you will return.

CHAPTER FIVE

Blackwater National Wildlife Refuge, Maryland : Waterfowl

*Understanding and drawing ducks and geese
at rest and in flight.*

C anada geese, ducks, and other waterfowl by the thousands spend the winter months on the Delmarva Peninsula. They arrive from northern Canada and flock into the ponds, rivers, and marshes beginning in early October. Residents feel that fall is upon them when they are awakened in the early morning by the honking of geese returning to seek their seasonal habitat. The trees are beginning to turn; the weather is becoming crisp. Skeins of geese circle and glide, their wings spread, web feet jutting out, descending to landings on the gray–cerulean blue waters of the Chesapeake Bay that reflect the reds, yellows, and oranges of the landscape.

One of the popular refuges for this waterfowl migration lies but a few miles southwest of Cambridge, Maryland. You can see geese and ducks all year long at Blackwater National Wildlife Refuge, but in the fall, additional hundreds—or, more likely, thousands—descend into the area and, with the colorful background of trees and marsh grasses, make it one of the great places to view the yearly ritual—and to paint and study the birds. In addition to Canada geese, there are snow geese, whistling swans, and more than twenty species of duck, along with ospreys, great blue herons, egrets, bald eagles, and more.

Cambridge is twelve or fourteen miles due south of Easton, just across the Choptank River. Once in Cambridge, heading east on U.S. 50, watch for Woods Road (there is a traffic light there), and turn right. This is a shortcut to Maryland Route 16 south, where you turn right again. (If you miss the Woods Road shortcut, your next light on Route 50 will be Maryland 16 south, where there is a large brown sign directing you to turn right to Blackwater National Wildlife Refuge.)

In either event, proceed south on Maryland 16 to the village of Church Creek and then turn left on Route 335. You will be driving through a sparsely populated countryside, where wood lots alternate with fields of soybeans, turning brown, ready to be harvested, and acres of milo—a kind of sorghum—with characteristic rich brown seedpods standing above the dark olive-green and yellowing sea of leaves. After a few miles, you will see a sign indicating Blackwater NWR off to your left. Turning on Key Wallace Drive, you will soon come upon the Visitors' Center. Information on the refuge, the drive, scenic vantage points, and walking trails is available to acquaint you with the area. Be sure to acquire a map of the drive through the refuge. There is a small admission fee per car, payable as you enter the refuge itself from the state road, a mile or so beyond the Visitors' Center.

The day I made the sketches and painted the watercolors in this chapter, I first drove the entire length of the Wildlife Drive loop to study the

scenery. There is so much to see, and I wanted to pick a suitable spot in which to set up my gear.

There were bushes and trees, marshes and tidal ponds, recently harvested fields of corn, and distant woodlands. Hundreds of geese were flying overhead and lounging on the quiet waters. I stopped often to look and savor the marshscape. After making the complete circuit, I returned to the entrance for a second drive-through. I had noted that location 8 on the map I had gotten at the Visitors' Center offered two scenes worth sketching and painting, so I set up there. The view to the left, across the warm-colored marsh, with reds and greens interrupted here and there with channels of bright, quiet water and a stand of loblolly pines in the background, struck me as a typical Blackwater scene. To the right, on the other side of the road, was another great composition. Several trees in the left foreground provided a frame, adding depth to the vista beyond, and the landscape was appealing. Both scenes allowed sufficient space in the sky to insert a few flying geese or ducks.

The first painting (color plate 5) is of the scene off to the right. I used a Winsor & Newton, 140-pound, 12″ × 16″ hot press block paper. I like this size for outdoor painting. It is large enough to be taken seriously, but small enough to let me finish painting a scene in a reasonable amount of time. An hour to an hour and a half puts me well into the painting. If that's all the time I have, the weather is changing, or I'm getting tired, I can always finish the watercolor in the studio.

The birds come next.

I don't even try to paint geese and ducks in detail. Paintings of game birds for stamps are, indeed, rendered in great detail, but in the field such minutia are often not even visible. What I try to do is to paint the birds as they appear in flight—impressions, really, of flying birds. Although waterfowl are often the center of interest in my paintings, my aim is to paint a representational landscape using the birds as an integral part of the composition. *Mates for Life,* I think, achieves this.

Wildfowl are skittish. Unless you are in a blind (or in a car), you usually cannot observe them from a close distance. They will glide away quietly and, if disturbed, take off, leaving you frustrated. But there are ways around this. Binoculars, of course, come in very handy. A telephoto lens on your camera is also a big help—though its benefit comes later, after the film is processed. In the field, without benefit of this equipment, I have found that you can learn to use your eyes like a camera. Watch the birds in flight and abruptly close your eyes, then open them and sketch what you have just seen. Repeat this as many times as you need to. My technique is to sketch the birds on a separate sheet of paper, a drawing tablet, and make many drawings. Because you can't get close to them and because they tend to move about, you must sketch rather quickly. You will also notice that ducks flap their wings much faster than geese and are thus more of a challenge to sketch.

There are several ways to view birds up close. One way is to seek out the domestic varieties. Often on a farm pond, for example, the ducks and

1

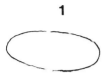

2

3

4

5

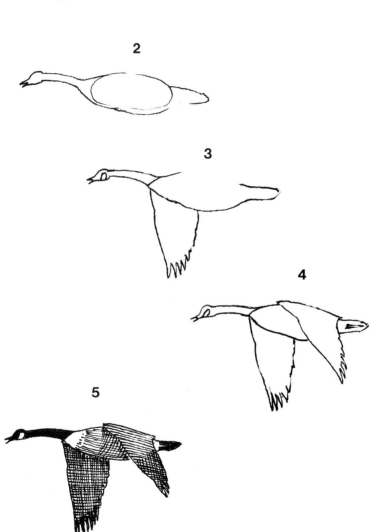

GEESE

DUCKS

GREAT BLUE HERON

geese are fed. This tends to make them tame and less fearful of people. You can then move closer in and sketch them in more detail. (At Blackwater, of course, putting out bait is not allowed.) Another way is to visit your local zoo. Here you can take your time and come in rather close simply because the birds cannot move away. Yet another method is to seek out a taxidermist; he or she will have specimens that can't move at all! And this brings up even another possibility—you can also benefit from examining the work of skilled carvers. Some carvings appear so real that you are tempted to clap your hands to see if they take flight. You might even consider making a carving yourself. You will learn more about bird anatomy and physiology than you thought you could know. I've tried it; it works.

Wherever you do your sketching, here are some tips to help you sketch Canada geese and some suggestions about painting them. As shown in the first drawing, I begin sketching the bird by drawing an oval for the body. Next, the head and neck, followed by an indication of chest and tail. I add the right wing in the third drawing, followed by the left wing. Notice that geese have "elbows" in their wings. In the fifth drawing I have shaded the bird. Almost always the light is from above and the wings will shade the body. I have also included a page of quick sketches of the geese as they lift off, fly overhead, or are paddling around.

Let me lead you through the steps of painting a Canada goose (color plate 6). In the first illustration I sketched the bird lightly, using raw umber on the body, and painted the bill, head, and neck black, leaving the characteristic white chin. In the second, I added black on the tail, leaving a slit of white in the center. I then painted the wings, using sepia. The light is from above. The right wing is thus in shadow, so I rendered it a bit darker, and I lifted a little color from the top of the left wing. In the third illustration, I added black at the tips of the wings and indicated feathers. I also introduced a cast shadow, a glaze of neutral tint, onto body. In number 4, I strengthened the shadows just a touch and added a

Plate 6. Painting Geese, 9" × 12"

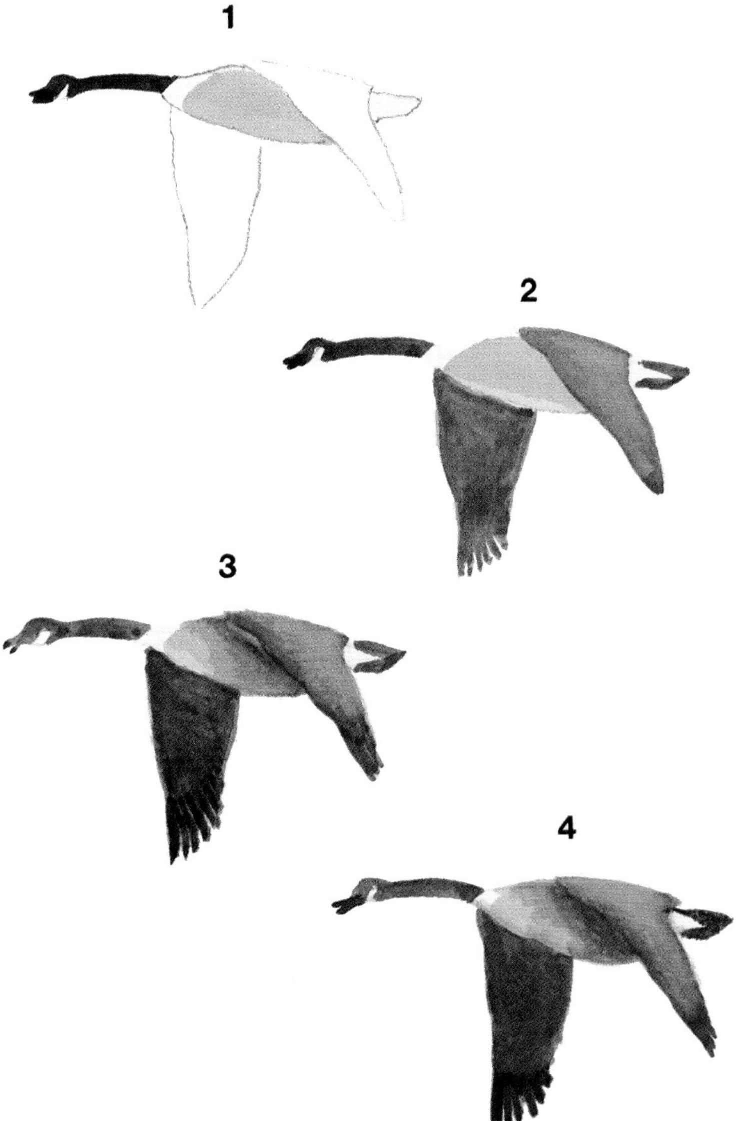

1

2

3

4

hint of cobalt blue under the white marking on the head and under the body.

In a detailed watercolor of two geese at rest, *Up Close and Personal,* I relied on close observation, sketches, and a wood carving. To confirm my own judgment, I often consult—as I did here—a good bird book. Such field guides can be very helpful, especially when the live creatures are so uncooperative and exact details are so difficult to see clearly.

The painting *Blackwater Marsh* is the view to the left at location 8 on the visitor's map—looking in the opposite direction from the earlier watercolor. I used a block of Lanaquarella 140-pound paper, 14" × 20". I started, as I usually do, with the sky and moved down the paper. For this painting, I wanted a cold, late fall feeling, and I achieved this through the treatment of the sky. The far trees were dark and the marsh golden, thanks to the blooming black-eyed susans. Burnt sienna, yellow ochre,

Blackwater Marsh,
14" × 20"

cadmium red, sepia, and a touch of sap green captured the bright, rich hues in front of me. The foreground water repeats, in the painting as in nature, the colors of the sky. Cerulean blue and neutral tint are two of my favorite colors with which to invoke the feel of early fall. The marsh grass reflections require a blend of alizarin crimson and viridian. These two take on a purple tint and, when blended with burnt sienna, make a great reflection, helping to make the painting a unified composition. The Canada geese are the last things to be added to the painting. I worked from my sketches, carefully placing the birds in the sky. I quite arbitrarily used seven geese and composed them as if I had just caught them in flight.

Obviously there is a risk in this method. You will have spent several hours on your landscape, marshscape, or whatever, and you don't want to ruin it. Now you purposely jeopardize the whole effort by inserting birds in the sky—and once committed to it, you cannot turn back. Just to gain some confidence, try a practice run or two. Paint a few birds on a piece of scrap paper. This will not only help confirm the scale of the birds in relation to the overall painting, but also relieve some of the tension, and you can then move on into the painting with assurance.

CHAPTER SIX

Deal Island, Maryland : Composition

Recognizing positive and negative space in a painting.
Balance and areas of a painting to be wary of.
The effects of leveling and sharpening in a composition.

eal Island, Maryland, is the locale of our next visit, and in this chapter we explore the fascinating subject of composition. Deal Island is situated southwest of Salisbury, overlooking Tangier Sound, which in turn is separated from the Chesapeake Bay by Bloodsworth, Smith, and several other marshy islands standing off the Eastern Shore. To reach Deal Island, you drive south from Salisbury on Route 13 to Princess Anne, where you then turn right (west) on Maryland 363, which, after about fifteen miles, deposits you on Deal. Like so much of the lower Shore, the scenery is flat—an expanse of marsh grass and scrub pines. The water table in this area is high, and there is almost always standing water at the sides of the road. You will even notice that, in the little grave-yards you pass, most of the burial vaults are above ground. As you approach open water, you come upon the little town of Chance. Over the bridge, just past the town, you are on Deal Island. Once there, the road meanders down the island, taking unexpected twists and turns, skirting around houses and churches with graveyards.

Among the churchyards you will pass is the one where Joshua Thomas is buried. A sign tells us that he was "the Parson of the Islands," a true missionary who, in the late eighteenth and early nineteenth centuries, almost single-handedly brought Methodism to the lower Eastern Shore of Maryland and Virginia and to the islands of the Chesapeake Bay. He traveled by skiff from one little church or camp meeting to another and was incessant in his zeal. The myriad Methodist churches throughout the region are a testament to his success.

The winding road eventually brings you to the small village of Wenona, at the southern tip of the island. It is only about three or four miles from the bridge to the tip of the island, though it seems farther. Once in Wenona, turn into the car park at the first basin, on the left. You will have gone about as far as you can go.

Across the basin lies Shirley and Linda's Shack. Often a skipjack or two will be tied up to the bulkhead. The Shack is a great subject in its own right. Including it in a scene with all the clutter along the pier and the skipjacks and workboats tied up nearby is virtually irresistible.

Like almost all of the small towns and villages on the Bay, this one is solely dependent on the water for its livelihood. This creates a special kind of landscape—one that I find completely fascinating and fresh, no matter how many variations of it I see. There are not only pilings and piers and slips and hoists, but also workboats tied up here and there (despite the ones that are missing on any given day, out working the Bay), along with the usual waterfront clutter—crab traps, marking buoys, bushel baskets, oyster tongs, and pieces of broken gear. There are buildings of various kinds, many of which extend over the water, supported by pilings, often with odd pieces of equipment, old ropes, and whatnot hanging off them. There are what is left of small boats and old cars. And there are the inevitable telephone poles and wires running here and there. Wherever you look, there is a sketchable, paintable scene.

IN COMPOSING a painting, an artist almost instinctively makes judgments that affect its composition. Among the elements you take into consideration are balance and space relationships. Space may be positive or negative. Objects can be thought of as positive space, whereas the areas surrounding objects are negative space.

There is an adage that says if the arrangement of the objects in a painting *looks* right, then it must *be* right. What is usually meant by this is that pleasing arrangements seem to be those in which certain compositional principles are observed. In this chapter, I want to describe and demonstrate some of these principles.

This is not to suggest that there are set rules you must follow. On the contrary, I don't think there are such rules. In fact, for every rule of composition that you can find—and you can surely find lists of them—I can find for you at least one outstanding work of art that defies it. However, there clearly are some guiding principles that will help you create pleasing arrangements. In the broadest sense, the skillful employment of these principles is the art of composition.

A satisfying painting has a center of interest. The viewer's eye goes fairly promptly to this along a guided visual path that the artist has created. More often than not, this path will then lead away from the center of interest to other areas of the painting, will cause the viewer to notice other parts of the arrangement, and will ultimately return to the center of interest. There are numerous routes for this visual path, and a few have been found to be particularly effective. Let me illustrate them.

In the first drawing, to simplify the discussion, I divided the plain pa-

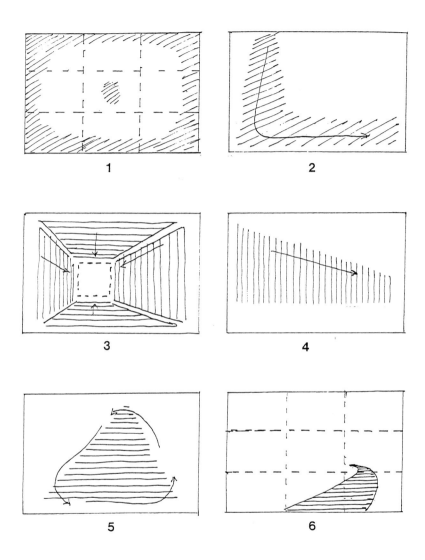

1
2
3
4
5
6

per into nine equal parts by marking it off into thirds both vertically and horizontally. I shaded the areas where you should avoid placing the center of interest. Should that center of interest be on the perimeter of the painting, there is the danger that the viewer's eye will be led off the edge and will not find its way back. Paradoxically, the middle of the area—the center—is also to be avoided. Why? Because when the center of interest is indeed at the center of the painting, the result is apt to be static rather than vital. Never say never, but it is safer to avoid these areas.

The other drawings, in diagram form, suggest some comfortable routes for the visual path to take. Drawing 2 illustrates the L arrangement. This is characterized by a strong vertical on one side of the painting, above and in combination with a strong horizontal.

The vertical thrust invites the eye to move up and down, as does a diagonal. This eye movement or agitation is called *sharpening,* and it has an active, restless, dynamic effect on the viewer. The opposite is true of leveling. *Leveling* describes the phenomenon of a horizontal emphasis in a composition, one that has a subtle, serene, and restful effect. Sharpening, then, sets up active eye movements; leveling soothes the traveling eye. The two are combined in an L arrangement, where obviously the vertical can be on either side and, indeed, can consist of more than one object.

Drawing 3 shows a tunnel, using four planes to lead the eye emphatically into the painting and to the center of interest, which is slightly off the true center. This is a powerful arrangement, often used in architectural settings. Wherever the eye goes, it comes back to the point of interest. Drawing 4 is more subtle. It illustrates a diagonal arrangement—looking down the road, for example—which draws the eye inexorably down toward the horizontal, from whence it returns, only to repeat the cycle.

Drawing 5, a triangle, is a favorite for group portraits and still lifes. A circle, which might be used for a flower arrangement, is very similar. Both shapes create a circular eye path for the viewer, aided by color and value.

Drawing 6 represents a classic, sweeping curve. This, too, is a powerful guide for eye movement and will point unequivocally to a center of

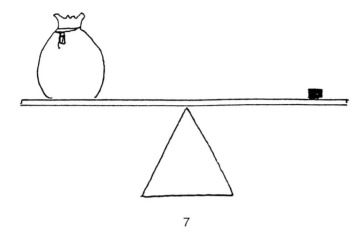

7

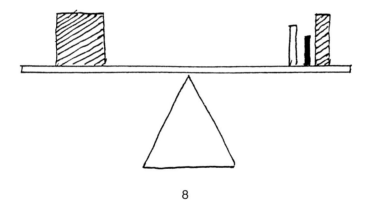

8

interest. I positioned this example in the nine-space grid to illustrate simultaneously another suggestion, to keep the rural road in your painting at the bottom of your composition. The extent to which it is less horizontal, or higher, is the extent to which it will look like a bird's-eye diagram rather than a representation of the road you are trying to depict.

The last two drawings are indeed diagrams, but I hope they will dramatize aspects of balance. Thus far, the drawings have been demonstrating aspects of arrangements of shapes and spaces and have related to the center of interest and the guidance of eye movements. These last drawings relate to balance. Balance may be attained by manipulating size, color, value, position—any number of elements. For example, drawing 7 suggests that a pound of feathers (large size) may be balanced by a pound of lead so long as the lead is represented in a dramatic color. Here it is simply black. It could well be red. It could be any really strong color if that color is in striking contrast to the balance of the painting. On the other hand, a symmetrical balance is easier to see. If a pound of feathers sat on each end of the seesaw, however, there would be a static and lifeless unity. Far better, as represented in drawing 8, is an approximate symmetry where varied size, color, shape, and value are used to create an arrangement that is optically comfortable. Balance may be symmetrical or asymmetrical. Balance may be between the positive and negative spaces. Something that is dominant by virtue of size or color, for example, may be balanced by some other part of the composition that the eye finds comfortable; the eye will ease back and forth between them.

N O W that you have been introduced to some aspects of composition—balance, arrangement, the play of positive and negative space, the manipulation of color, size, shape, and value—we'll turn to the paintings made from sketches done on the most recent day I visited Deal Island.

The painting of *Shirley and Linda's Shack* is a good example of the L composition—in this instance, a reverse or backward L. The tall mast of the skipjack, extending into the sky, serves as the strong vertical. The hull of the boat, the bulkhead, and the Shack compose a strong horizontal, or leg of the L. Your eye goes first to Shirley and Linda's shack, which because of its size and color is the most prominent feature of the painting. Your eye then moves left to right, as it does when you read,

along the strong horizontal formed by the bulkhead and the white hull of the skipjack. Once out to the right edge of the painting, the guided visual path reverses course and goes up the standing rigging and the mast to the top and, from there, diagonally down and left along the clouds, back to the shack. The trail leads the eye in an all-encompassing loop. There is a comfortable balance between the negative space (the sky) and the activity along the whole bottom of the painting (positive space). In general, the L arrangement is a safe and commonly used composition. It is comfortable and, because it has a strong horizontal base, it is reassuring.

You should be careful, however, not to be heavy handed. If you use the L arrangement, for example, use it loosely, not to the exclusion of everything that doesn't fit strictly within the L pattern. We are not cameras. We can indeed modify the scene we are painting. We can move a telephone pole or omit it altogether. We can add or subtract a boat at the dock, and we do these things to "improve" the composition, but you

Plate 7. Patent Tonger,
12" × 16"

should avoid simplifying to the point that only a vertical and a horizontal axis are left. The decisions about what to keep in a painting and what to eliminate should not be made casually, but only after judicious thought.

The painting of the Shack successfully demonstrates the L arrangement and avoids oversimplification. I omitted nothing significant, and this brings up another point worth remembering. Viewers enjoy recognizing a location or place that they have visited. This suggests that, if you paint a well-known scene—or, I should say, a scene of a well-known place—you are obliged to be fairly faithful in your rendition lest you run the risk of not being credible.

Patent Tonger (color plate 7) offers an example of sharpening—a composition using diagonals, as illustrated in drawing 4. The diagonal pier and the diagonal lines of the rigging of the workboat stimulate the viewer's eye movement. To balance these, I arranged the clouds in a diagonal as well, this time from upper right to lower left. As usual, I painted the sky first, then addressed the distant marshes, followed by the townhouses and the long shed in the middle ground. For the townhouses, I used violet, cerulean blue, and a touch of neutral tint. For the long shed, cerulean blue and neutral tint again, but this time with some sepia. The pilings under the shed are silhouetted against a light background using sepia and Prussian blue. Then I turned to the boat, *Swamp Fox*. I retained the white of the paper for the bright parts of the hull and cabin, but used cerulean blue and a touch of black for the shaded side of the boat, spars, engine box, and baskets on the stern. I also introduced a little violet on the shaded hull to echo the violet in the townhouses. Then I used the local colors of the small items on the boat—the baskets, boxes, and tongs. Then the spars of the tonging rig.

You have to observe carefully to portray accurately the spars and rigging. If you are in doubt of the function of a line, for example, go closer and take a look. Every line and cable, every boom and spar and block, has a specific purpose, and it is imperative that you understand them well enough to get them right.

The water and reflections were painted last. The reeds and grasses in the foreground were done with gouache. (I will describe this in the next chapter.) To keep the reeds distinctly close, one must make them opaque.

Fall at Deal Island is a quiet, restful view of the waterfront area. I began the painting with the sky, working from the horizon up. The weather was warm, and I began with a warm tint, yellow ochre with a touch of ivory black—just a touch. I added little dabs of neutral tint as I worked my way up the paper to the top. I stroked in cerulean blue, on a slight diagonal, moving from the upper right to the lower left. The overall effect depicts a warm, hazy day.

The buildings in the background came next. The various shapes, poles, and trees are kept light, keeping them in the background. Next, the white fishing shack, the pier, and the skipjack mast on the left. The shadows under the shack and pier are kept dark and transparent. Final-

Fall at Deal Island,
12" × 16"

ly, I painted the grass in the foreground and the waterman just to the right of the shack. A figure, even an incidental figure, draws the eye to it and not only adds a sense of scale, but also provides a human touch.

The foreground requires as much attention as any other segment of the painting. Many painters, to their peril, slough off the foreground or give it short shrift. I feel that the foreground deserves detail and concentration, especially when it is water and reflections—but more about that later. The vertical mast at the left brings the eye down to the ground level, then the eye moves left to right along the dark underside of the fishing shack and along the base of the pier, then up the second mast to the sky and diagonally down the blue brush strokes, back to the mast where we began. The visual path is restful and pleasing.

The guided visual path is very important. Eye movement is so subtle that one is rarely aware of it. If it is disrupted, however, or jarring, the viewer may take an instant dislike to the painting, perhaps not even knowing why. Poor judgment on the part of the artist in drawing, composition, color, or even the handling of the medium can create havoc to the eye.

DEAL ISLAND may seem to be the end of the road, but it abounds in subject matter for the artist or photographer. There are sketches and paintings to be made, scenes to be captured, wherever you look. If you want to go to the end of a road to paint, this is a good one to go to the end of.

CHAPTER SEVEN

Crisfield and Smith Island, Maryland : Color

Understanding color. The color wheel and the mixing of colors. The role of color in perspective.

The importance of color in a painting is impossible to overemphasize. To debate whether it is more important than composition or subject matter is to debate which is the most important leg of a three-legged stool.

How you react to specific colors is subjective and depends largely on personal preferences, often developed through experience. But your reaction to the phenomenon of color itself is pretty basic, and the appeal of a particular painting is frequently heightened by the color choices the artist has made, quite apart from its subject matter. A bright, colorful, clean painting among dark, somber, low-key ones will often dominate an exhibit—on the appeal of color alone.

Each artist, in the course of time and with the accumulation of experience, develops a palette, by which I mean a selection of specific colors with which to paint, to his or her liking, and tends to stick with it. Often this palette helps define a particular artist's work and becomes virtually as recognizable as a signature.

The aim of this chapter is to help you understand color. Perhaps I can assist in the development of a palette with which you feel comfortable and suggest ways in which these selections of colors may be used effectively to strengthen your composition and perspective.

WHEN WE PAINT OUTDOORS, the sun is our light source, and its light includes the whole spectrum. Without attempting to explain the physics of light, let me just say that the *color* of an object is that spectral part of the sun's light that is reflected by the object. The color we perceive, or see—another complex phenomenon that we needn't go into here—is that reflected segment of the spectrum. Not all light, of course, is the same, and the *quality* of the particular light falling on an object affects, if not determines, the hue, the intensity, and even the value of the colors you see. *Hue* is the specific color; *intensity* is, essentially, its purity; and *value* is its saturation. These terms will become clearer as we go along.

You will have noticed that sunlight in the early hours of the day is fresh and cool, whereas the late afternoon sun casts a warm glow over the landscape. In the midday sun, colors are sharp and vivid, and the contrast is high. Conversely, the light on a cloudy day is less intense and tends to soften colors. A fog or a haze affects the light and thus the colors you see. The colors in the same vista will look different from one day to the next, from one time of day to another, and so forth. A good example of how different a particular scene can look when painted at different times of the day is the series of paintings by Monet of his famous haystack.

Indoors, artificial light is something else again. Incandescent bulbs produce a very warm light, much warmer even than sunlight at the end of the day. Most fluorescent lights, on the other hand, give a cool, greenish blue cast. In your studio, it might be wise to do as most galleries do by creating a mixture of warm and cool illumination. The combination of incandescent and fluorescent lights will not duplicate sunlight, but will be better than either kind by itself.

Acknowledging that the quality of light affects colors, we nevertheless paint what we see, and what we see at a given time and under given conditions is the local color—the light reflected by the subject.

In 1874 a group of about thirty artists, whose unconventional work had been rejected by the French Salon, held their own exhibition in the studio of the photographer Félix Nadar. The reviewers of this show, seeking to characterize this new school of painting, coined the term *impressionism,* and the name stuck. What the critics saw were paintings in which the artists did not analyze the forms of their subjects so much as respond to the colors reflected by these forms. The paintings comprised arrays of color—the effects of reflected light—and these colors invited the eye to define the forms being portrayed. That the painters were concentrating on myriad light stimuli rather than on "things" was a revolutionary concept, a complete turnabout from the classic, representational painting style then in vogue.

I am not a purist with respect to impressionism, but I mention it to emphasize that you will do well to respond to color as well as form and to capture both as accurately as you see them.

N O W, let's turn to the colors themselves. We learned in grade school that there are three primary colors—red, yellow, and blue. In painting, however, and in working with pigments and their combinations, it is clearer

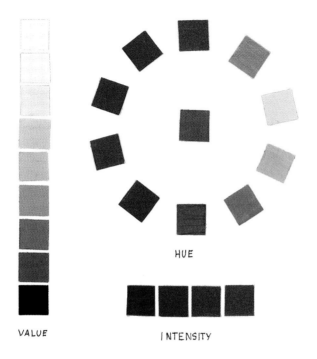

HUE

VALUE

INTENSITY

Plate 8. The color wheel shows us hue. Value is demonstrated at the left, and intensity is shown at the bottom.

if we think in terms of five primaries: red, yellow, green, blue, and violet. Going one step further, we add the in-between colors: orange, yellow-green, blue-green, blue-violet, and red-violet. Now we have created a ten-color range, or spectrum, not unlike the spectrum that results when, by using a prism, sunlight is separated into its component parts. Instead of visualizing this spectrum as a linear bar, however, as a prism reveals it, think of it in the form of a circle—a color wheel. (See color plate 8.)

Each color in a color wheel is the complementary color to the one directly opposite it. Thus, the complement of red is blue-green, the complement of yellow is blue-violet, and so forth. These relationships will become increasingly important to you as you work with colors, and it is not a bad idea to memorize the ten colors in the color wheel so you almost instinctively know which is the complementary color of each color.

In the center of the wheel is a brown patch. This is the color you get by mixing two complementary colors about equally. This example is a fairly clean color, but if you should mix a whole bunch of colors, you would get a murky mud pie. You should remember this. The mud pie effect will occur on your palette itself if you mix one color after another—usually by mixing in more hues in an attempt to modify the color you seem to be getting. And it will surely appear in your painting when you overcorrect—when you go back over an area several times in an effort to "improve" it. This muddying is to be avoided, both on your palette and in your work.

While overworking is to be avoided, mixing of colors, of course, is not. On the contrary, unless you intend to be limited to the colors in your paint box, you must mix them to create other hues.

The *brightest* hues will be those directly from the tube or pan and those created by mixing or combining those that are adjacent to each other on the color wheel. Adding colors to each other, while it will change the colors, does not make them brighter.

To tone down, or *dull*, a color, add a little of its complementary color. This dulling effect is demonstrated in the intensity, or chroma, scale in plate 8, which begins on the right with the pure color red. To this red I added some blue-green in gradual steps, with the red becoming duller each time. There is a profound difference between dulling a color (which this scale demonstrates) and *darkening* a color (which is achieved by adding black).

To *lighten* a color you simply charge your brush with clean water and pick up only a relatively small amount of pigment in your brush. This creates a thin glaze, or wash, allowing the white paper to show through the transparent paint, lightening the color.

In the concept of five basic and five in-between colors, black is not

considered a color, nor is white. Black and white are values. Although, as I have pointed out, black is used to darken a color, lightening a color does not (however logical it seems to be) involve the use of white. In fact, if you mix white with transparent watercolor, the paint becomes opaque. Opaque watercolor is called *gouache* (rhymes with *wash*). Pure transparent watercolor—*aquarelle*—does not permit the use of white. On the other hand, sometimes it is necessary to go back into a painting and add white to areas that were inadvertently painted over. I have done it, and it is acceptable in most cases. Some art shows allow only pure aquarelle, and in many open shows a special prize is offered for the best all-transparent watercolor.

Notice that plate 8 includes value and intensity scales. The value scale shows nine progressive steps from white to black. This is an unusually difficult scale to paint, and you should try it at least once. Use any medium you want—gouache, oil, acrylic. This one was done with tempera paints. I occasionally paint an all black-and-white painting, using all

Winsor and Newton $^1/_2$ Pan Watercolor Box, Twenty-two Colors

1	alizarin crimson	12	Hooker's green light
*2	bright red	13	Winsor green
*3	cadmium red	*14	cobalt blue
4	cadmium red deep	*15	cerulean blue
*5	Van Dyke brown	*16	Prussian blue
*6	burnt sienna	17	Winsor blue
*7	burnt umber	18	Winsor violet
*8	yellow ochre	19	Paynes' gray
9	Indian yellow	*20	neutral tint
*10	sap green	*21	ivory black
11	Hooker's green	22	Chinese white

*Author's preferred colors

nine values, as an exercise to refresh my value interpretation of a subject. It is good practice.

Henlopen Anchorage is an example of a *value painting* limited to black and white; this case was also limited to a single brush, a one-half inch flat.

As far as your palette is concerned, you do not need a host of colors to paint a painting. Anywhere from six to twelve choice colors will probably suffice. You will come to develop your own selection. I list here the colors that make up the twenty-two color Winsor & Newton pan box, with asterisks indicating the nine colors I favor and tend to use almost exclusively. Even if my paint box had more hues available, I would never use all of them. I find myself replacing the same few colors each year. My prediction is that you will do the same.

TO ILLUSTRATE the role of color in perspective, I went to Smith Island, a marvelously picturesque spot that almost seems to have been caught in the web of time at some earlier era. It lies in the Chesapeake Bay, straddling the Maryland-Virginia state line roughly a dozen miles west, across Tangier Sound, from Crisfield, Maryland. Crisfield, in turn, is about thirty miles below Salisbury. You take U.S. 13 south from Salis-

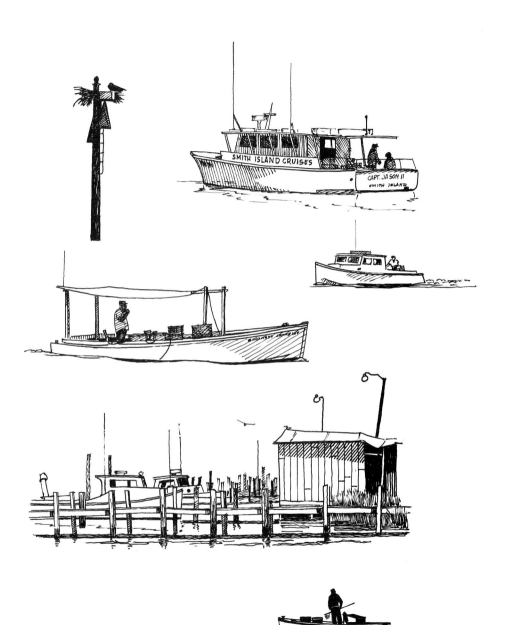

Plate 9. Cool colors recede, and warm colors advance.

bury for some seventeen miles, then Maryland 413, through the village of Marion, another fourteen miles to Crisfield. Much of the road is straight as a string. It often has standing water in the ditches on either side, and the flat landscape is what you have seen before on the Eastern Shore: cultivated fields, stands of loblolly pines, and marshes—but little else.

Crisfield, on the other hand, is a small, bustling community, entirely dependent on the Bay. It probably has more crab and oyster processing businesses than any other town on the Eastern Shore. Wharves, workboats, and packing houses dominate the waterfront, and there seems always to be activity on the water. At the end of Main Street is a large public pier, with a pavilion, from which you can look back at part of the town as if from the Bay itself. It is from this pier that mail boats leave for both Tangier and Smith Islands. There are cruise boats, too, but that's something else. The mail boat is the boat to get so that you can be on your own on the island rather than being part of a tour. Mail boats to Smith Island go to one or the other of two villages on Smith, Ewell or Tylerton, and occasionally a boat will go to both. It is a simple matter to ask. From Memorial Day through mid-October, the boats leave Crisfield at 12:30— just after noon—and return, leaving Smith Island at 4 o'clock. They make another trip at 5:00 P.M., staying overnight at the island and re-turning to Crisfield the next morning to begin the cycle again. The trip, traveling at about sixteen knots, takes thirty-five or forty minutes. The current cost is a modest fifteen dollars for the round trip.

On this particular occasion, I arrived early enough to be able to park (free) right at the pier. I took the 12:30 boat from Crisfield to Ewell. It was a sweltering day, but the "voyage" was a delight. The mail boat was piled high with boxes of all sorts of groceries and other supplies for the islanders, and I assume it also carried the mail! There were five other pas-sengers. I returned in the afternoon.

The advantages of the one-day excursion are apparent. The disadvan-tages are that you have a severely limited time on Smith Island, and the midday light is rather harsh. (And, on the day I went, it was well above ninety degrees, as well.) There are several bed-and-breakfast establish-ments, both in Ewell and in Tylerton, so staying over is easy and would allow you not only more time, but more pleasant conditions in which to paint than I found on this trip.

WE ALL KNOW that things at a distance look hazier and less distinct than things in the middle ground. And things in the middle ground are less sharp than objects closest to you. This is virtually irrespective of their local colors. But color itself can be used to emphasize or create a sense of distance or perspective. The basic thing to remember about the use of color in perspective is that distant objects not only are less dis-tinct, but also take on a blue haze, whereas objects close to you have a warmer tone. Putting this another way, cool colors recede and warm col-

Plate 10. Workboat
Basin, Smith Island,
10" × 16"

ors advance. To dramatize this fundamental thesis, I prepared color plate 9: a yellow circle on a blue background and another with blue on yellow. You will easily see that the small yellow circle almost jumps into your lap and the small blue circle falls back beneath the page. Well, almost.

To illustrate this phenomenon in a painting, I chose a view of the workboat basin in Ewell (color plate 10). First finding a spot in the shade of a waterman's shack as a place to work, I set up my little stool and my gear and made a rather complete sketch. I then wet the sky area with clear water until I had an even dampness. Then, painting from the horizon up, I mixed a warm color comprising cadmium yellow and a touch of cerulean blue. In the upper half of the sky, I painted the underside of the clouds with neutral tint. Being careful to hold the white of the clouds, I painted the blue sky with cerulean blue.

The middle ground of the composition, a row of fishing shacks and sloughing pens (which will be explained in the next chapter), was painted with a wash of neutral tint and cobalt blue. This allowed—no, it forced—the buildings to recede into the distance. After this was dry, I painted each shack and roof a different tint. The workboat was kept white, and the pilings in the foreground were painted with a warm burnt sienna and yellow ochre, each with a light and dark side. The rowboat and the pier were kept warm in color. Lines, textures, reflections, and some details were then added.

Water reflects that which is above, so the water here was painted with the same colors that were used in the sky. A few small waves and a shadow under the pier completed the painting. I confess that, because my time on Smith Island was limited and the day was stifling, I actually completed only the sketch itself on the spot, finishing the painting later in the studio with the memory aid of a couple of photographs.

Abandoned Fishing Shack was done completely from a photograph tak-

Abandoned Fishing
Shack, *12" × 16"*

en that day. It was one of a dozen or so scenes I recorded for future reference. There are a number of fishing shacks roosting on pilings around Smith Island, and a few of them appear to be abandoned. Again I used cool colors to depict the parts of the scene that are distant and warm colors, strong and with some detail, for the foreground.

CHAPTER EIGHT

Saxis, Virginia : Texture

*Using the drybrush to create texture. Illustrating the
illusion of texture on a surface.*

Landscape painting always presents an array of challenges. We have already dealt with some of them—drawing, perspective, composition, value, and color. We are now going to move into the area of technique, where there is much to explore.

In this chapter we visit the bayside village of Saxis, Virginia. This little dot on the map is just east of Crisfield, Maryland—probably not more than ten miles as the gull flies—but it's about fifty miles by car and is across the state line, in Virginia. South from Salisbury on U.S. Route 13, you reach the state line after about thirty miles. Within the first two miles in Virginia, there is a welcome station where you can pick up a good map. In another three miles you pass the turnoff to Chincoteague (about which more in chapter 10), and about eight miles into the state, as you enter the town of Temperanceville, you must watch for an insignificant sign marking, off to the right, Virginia Route 695. This secondary road heads west for roughly eleven miles before it ends at the water's edge in Saxis.

Saxis is not a tourist town. On the contrary, it is strictly a waterman's village, with no frills. It consists of small houses, wharves, a workboat basin, and a group of sloughing sheds and packing houses. The sloughing sheds, themselves often on pilings next to a dock, contain troughs or bins perhaps ten or twelve feet long, four feet wide, and a foot deep. These are built on trestles about three feet off the deck. Depending on the size of the operation, there could be dozens of these bins, end to end, often in rows two bins wide with walkways between. Some are within a shed, and others are on piers out over the water. Each has water piped in and a drain so that the water in each bin, about six inches deep, is constantly refreshed. The point of all this is to harvest soft-shelled crabs, and work in the sloughing sheds is thus a summertime activity. (In the winter, the harvest is oysters.)

When blue crabs, those famous inhabitants of the Chesapeake Bay, outgrow their shells, as they do several times during their lifetimes, they molt. They burst out of their confinement and within a matter of hours begin to develop a new and larger shell. In the meantime, they are soft-shells—looking every bit like a standard crab, color and all, but soft to the touch and totally helpless. Soft-shells are extremely vulnerable to their various predators—among whom are those of us who salivate just thinking of them. When they are about to molt, the crabs develop a telltale pinkness on their rear legs. Watermen can spot these peelers, as the about-to-shed crabs are called, about as far away as they can see them. It is the peelers, then, that are placed in the sloughing bins and monitored every couple of hours, day and night, for their metamorphosis into soft-shells. Since crabs will eat each other when they are defenseless, they must be removed as soon as they lose their old shells.

Because soft-shelled crabs are such delicacies, they command good prices and are obviously worth all this trouble. But enough of this. Back to Saxis and to painting.

For painters, the point of going to Saxis is to see the basin, piers, different sorts of workboats, packing houses, sloughing sheds, piles of oyster shells, pickups, and refrigerated trucks being loaded for market. This is a working community. Unless you are working, buying, or painting, there is little reason to be in Saxis.

TEXTURE is the aspect of painting that gives the illusion of a tactile surface and, when successfully rendered, gives the viewer a sensation of what the surface actually feels like. While close approximation of dark and light patterns is an important part of suggesting texture, it is not uncommon to simulate specific textures. The painter has a variety of techniques from which to choose—drybrush, scratching or spreading with a knife, flicking or spattering, or, indeed, careful, detailed painting.

In color plate 11 I have shown how to create a drybrush effect in watercolor. I suggest that, certainly at the beginning, you try this only on a cold press, rough-surface paper. It is the texture of the sheet—the minute mountains and valleys—that makes this technique possible. (Hot press paper is comparatively smooth and almost polished.) Start by applying local color to the object to be textured and allowing it to dry thoroughly. Then, using a flat brush charged with pigment that is darker than the local color and just a *little* water, drag the brush quickly across the surface, holding the handle of the brush almost parallel to the paper. This quick stroke allows the paint to hit only the mountaintops of the paper's surface, leaving the valleys unaffected. Obviously, you should do this quickly and firmly and not go back over it. Going back would tend to fill in the valleys, simply changing the local color without suggesting any

Plate 11. Textures, 10" × 12"

LOCAL COLOR

DRYBRUSH

FLICKING WITH A TOOTHBRUSH

BOARD AND BATTEN

PILINGS AND BULKHEAD

SCRATCHED

PAINTED

GRASS, TWIGS, AND STICKS

texture. Drybrush works well in a number of situations. Piers and bulkheads, for example, weathered by sun and water, are good candidates for this treatment. And there are others.

On either a rough-surface cold press paper or a smooth hot press paper, you can use a knife to scratch or score lines. The wet paint will flow into these scratches, concentrating the pigment and producing dark lines. Siding or clapboards on houses and grass and twigs are often rendered this way. By using the blade of a knife, as if spreading butter on bread, a damp area may be partially lifted—that is, some of the paint removed—to produce a lighter local color. The illustration of grass includes this effect.

In *The Red Shed* (color plate 12), textures are integral. The shed, near the workboat basin in Saxis, is not too much in itself, but the outside stairs and particularly the striking shadows they cast caught my eye. The red building was also a nice contrast to the white boat stranded, high and dry, by the low tide.

First, of course, I made a pencil sketch and then began my painting with the sky. Saxis is hot in mid-July, and this day was no exception. The sky was clear. I wanted to emphasize this, so I wet the sky area and, starting on the right, painted a tint of gamboge with a touch of cerulean blue.

Plate 12. The Red Shed, *12" × 16"*

67

The colors were kept light to bring out the feeling of the summer day's sun. I then stroked in the background marshes and the water. These, too, were kept light in tone because they were in the hazy distance. For the shed, I used cadmium red medium, with a touch of sepia to dull and darken it, thus reinforcing the strong dark and light pattern. The edges of the panels on the shed were covered with battens. I put in their linear shadows, providing a little texture to the otherwise flat area. The shadows of the stairs were painted after the surface of the building had dried. The sloughing pens beyond were kept simple. From where I was, I could see none of their details, so I thought it best (always a smart thing to do) to paint what I saw: poles, horizontal boards, and a beautiful play of dark and light patterns.

I then turned to the grasses and the sand. I used sap green and added an occasional touch of cadmium yellow. I added texture to the sand by using the toothbrush-and-thumb technique and to the grass by using a small, round brush—and care.

ALTHOUGH it was painted in Lewes, Delaware, rather than in Saxis, I also include here a painting of the old Life Saving Station because it demonstrates several texture-creating techniques. By now you know that I sketch first and then begin painting the sky, working up from the horizon. I then work down from the horizon to the foreground.

The entire painting was done on the spot, on a bright morning. It was important to establish the dark-and-light pattern on the building as I had sketched it, before the sun moved too far—before the light changed. So I did, using a one-inch flat brush. Once I got everything blocked in, I turned my attention to the several textures. First, the board-and-batten siding. To render this effectively, you must pay attention to the cast shadows and shading on the battens. On the shadowed side of the building, the battens are lighter than those on the sunny side. This is, to some

The Old Life Saving
Station, *12" × 16"*

extent, an illusion, since I painted the boards between the battens with a
deeper shade.

For the gravel in the driveway, I used a toothbrush and my thumb. After masking the other areas of the painting, I dampened the toothbrush,
picked up some earthy pigment, and spattered it freely over the road
area. The masking is important. You can use almost anything—a facial
tissue, a paper towel, a plastic bag. Anything handy. Just be sure your
work is sufficiently dry so as not to smudge what you are trying to pro-
tect. This spattering technique is useful to render sand, gravel, or dirt.
Corot, as a matter of fact, used it to put specks of blue in the foreground
of some of his paintings, thus bringing the color of the sky lower into the
paintings.

The attention you pay to creating the illusion of texture in your paintings will contribute immeasurably to the finished works and to the enjoyment of those who view them.

Wachapreague, Virginia : Marshes

Working with greens.

Virginia's Eastern Shore consists of two counties, Accomack, which borders Maryland, and Northampton, which extends down to Cape Charles, helping to form the mouth of the Chesapeake Bay. Both counties have scores of tidal streams and inlets on the Bay side and are protected from the Atlantic on the other side by an almost continuous string of barrier islands. These islands consist of dunes and grasses, and many of them don't even have dunes, which is to say that they are marshes. With the exception of Chincoteague, which we visit in the next chapter, there are no communities on any of these marshy outposts.

Plate 13. No Wake,
12" × 16"

Well down in Accomack County, about thirty miles down U.S. 13 from the Maryland line, is the crossroads village of Keller at the intersection of east-west Virginia 180. To the right a few miles is the Chesapeake Bay; to the left about four miles is the small fishing village of Wachapreague, our current destination.

Wachapreague faces the broad, green marshes that extend for several miles to the east, beyond which are the open waters of the Atlantic Ocean. Charts indicate that boats must follow a meandering tidal waterway for four or five miles to reach the ocean. A wide variety of boats are tied up at the local piers. There are some pleasure boats, but most are small commercial fishing vessels, with an occasional large trawler. Most appear to be equipped to haul drift nets.

I WAS PARTICULARLY ANXIOUS to find a subject for a painting that would include the wonderful marsh (see color plate 13). The colors are so varied. There are bright greens, yellow-greens, blue-greens, dull

The Trawler,
15" × 22"

greens, and touches of red and yellow. And there are intriguing patterns—the array of greens in contrast to the silver and blue paths of water and the overarching sky. Sure enough, I wandered out on one of the many piers and spotted, across the way, an abandoned motorboat, left to die among the reeds and grasses of the marsh. I would have preferred to have been higher so I could have seen more of the waterways, with their pattern of twists and turns—but you must be content with what is available, and I was.

After a quick sketch I wet the sky and began. The morning sky was primarily warm, and I used cadmium yellow and yellow ochre, mixed. For the darker clouds, I used neutral tint and alizarin carmine, in various values, followed by cerulean blue in the upper left corner. The low islands in the distance were painted next, using a mixture of neutral tint and cerulean blue. For the marsh grasses in the middle ground, I added cadmium yellow to sap green in various quantities, along with touches of cobalt blue. A little of the neutral tint and alizarin carmine, used in the sky, was repeated here and there in the marsh. The touch of sky colors in the foreground tends, almost subconsciously, to add cohesion to the painting. I also added a few specks of bright yellow to represent blooming flowers among the grasses. And, although the water was quiet, I creased it a little to show some movement, but mostly to direct the eye toward the abandoned boat.

From the end of the same pier from which *No Wake* was sketched, looking hard right rather than directly ahead, was a completely different scene—and another captivating subject. Here, tied up to a bulkhead, was a good-sized trawler, perhaps a shrimper. Behind it were some buildings, including a restaurant from which you could overlook the area, and some piers. Beyond was a marina and more activity than appears here. Invoking my artistic license, I took the prerogative of simplifying that part of the scene and of extending the marsh area. I take these liberties only rarely, but it seemed the right thing to do here.

Trawlers are fascinating boats. They are designed to operate offshore, and all have a sharp sheer, a high freeboard, and a confusing array of spars and rigging. As on all workboats, the lines and standing rigging all have specific purposes. They begin in one place and end up in another. There are blocks through which many of the lines pass. You must not paint them willy-nilly, but must be as accurate as possible. In this instance I don't pretend to know the function of all the lines, but I do know what I see, and I try to portray what I see as accurately as possible. This takes time, but it is time well spent.

A word about rigging. Do not succumb to the temptation to use a ruler. When a nautical line is taut and, therefore, straight, you want to show it as straight. But if you use a ruler, the rigging will be stiff, artificial, and uninteresting. A freehand rendering is best—a good, steady freehand, that is.

Notice that I kept the water quiet in the background, which allows better reflection of the bright sun. The strong horizontal this creates is integral to the composition.

Chincoteague, Virginia : Wet into Wet

Wetting the paper to capture the soft look.
Painting the entire painting while the paper is wet.

Thanks to *Misty,* generations of children are aware of Chincoteague, but it is, of course, much more than the setting for a wonderful story of a pony. It is a small barrier island off the Virginia coast, and the town of the same name occupies virtually all of it.

Chincoteague lies about eight miles into Virginia from Maryland and about seven miles east of U.S. 13. The road to the island, Virginia 175, goes around Wallops Flight Facility, which is part of NASA, and across Chincoteague Bay on a causeway before going over a drawbridge onto the island. On the left, as you approach, is a string of billboards, quite uniform in size, about a hundred yards apart—regular as clockwork—

touting places to see, where to eat, and what to do when you get to Chincoteague. The view on the right side of the road is unspoiled, and you look out on endless marshes and the shallow waters of the bay. The town, at first appearing as a row of silhouetted buildings, becomes clearer as you get nearer, is picturesque, and offers some great subject matter for paintings along the active waterfront.

Once on the island, you will find that the town is much like many summer resort areas, replete with craft shops, art galleries, restaurants, T-shirt and curio stores, real estate offices, and other conveniences that cater to the tourists, campers, and trailer and motor home denizens that swell its summer population.

The biggest event of the year is the annual Pony Penning, held on the last Wednesday and Thursday of July. Members of the Chincoteague Volunteer Fire Company, who own the herd, round up the so-called Chincoteague ponies on nearby Assateague Island, swim them across the narrow inlet, pen them, and then auction off many of the foals. The proceeds help support the fire company. The event brings thousands of eager visitors.

In strong contrast to the hustle-bustle of this vibrant little town is its neighbor, Assateague Island. Assateague is a narrow island roughly twenty miles long, about half in Maryland and half in Virginia, most of it under the jurisdiction of the National Park Service as the Assateague Island National Seashore. On the Maryland end of the island is a state park. On the south end—right across a narrow waterway from Chincoteague Island—is the Chincoteague National Wildlife Refuge. The refuge is just a skip and a jump, and across a short bridge, from the town of Chincoteague. But as you go through the gate and enter the refuge, you enter a different world.

This sandy, marshy island is inhabited by myriad waterfowl, sika deer, Delmarva fox squirrels, and other creatures—a vast array of flora and fauna—plus a zillion or two mosquitoes. (It is essential, if you go between

Plate 14. Ponies Grazing, *12″ × 16″*

late spring and the first killing frost of the fall, that you bring insect repellent.) There is a wonderful, pristine beach, and there are drives and walking trails. The refuge is a mecca for birders, fishermen, naturalists, photographers, bikers and walkers, and others who love the great outdoors.

On this trip, after a leisurely tour through the refuge to assess my options, I took the Wildlife Loop. This offered a number of inviting scenes, but when I came across a little meadow where some wild ponies were feeding, I knew I had found my painting (color plate 14). I got out for a better look, but because of the heat and the ravenous mosquitoes I beat a quick retreat to my van. From the van I took several photographs and made a sketch. Later, in the comfort of my studio, I undertook the painting. Even if I hadn't fled the natural hazards, wet into wet painting almost has to be done indoors.

WET INTO WET watercolor can be exasperating, but it can be richly rewarding. Not only need it be done indoors, it must be painted in one sitting.

I like to work on a sturdy 140-pound paper, usually hot press. I find that cold press, for some subjects, works well because the paper accepts the paint more easily, but this is really a matter of personal choice. In any event, for *Ponies Grazing* I used a 140-pound hot press Arches paper. I first drew the scene lightly in pencil. Then I immersed the paper in the bathtub, which I had filled with enough water to cover the paper, and left it for about twenty minutes, until the paper was completely saturated. I then stapled it to my drawing board with staples all around at about three-inch intervals.

Once the paper was fast to the board, I used a three-inch brush and lifted some of the water. This is done by wetting the brush, squeezing as much water out of it as you can, and then drawing it across the surface of the paper. This picks up any "standing water" and, indeed, will pick up some of the pigment if you have already painted the area. In other words, lifting, frequently used to lighten a color, is here used merely to reduce the amount of water on the surface of the paper. You don't want the surface to be soupy, just good and damp.

I began painting with the sky and moved down the paper, letting the colors go where they might. I painted with care, but occasionally the paint seemed to go its own way more wildly than I had planned. If at any time you feel that the paint has gotten out of hand, if the color is too intense or has spread too widely, you can lift the "mistake" with a damp brush and continue painting.

You will have noticed in earlier chapters that often, not to say usually, as I begin a landscape painting I first dampen the sky area and thus paint the sky and clouds with a modified wet into wet technique. I say *modified* because usually only the surface of the paper is dampened, and only dampened—not saturated. The purpose of both of these methods is to let the edges of areas bleed softly off into nothingness. Hard edges are avoided. This is particularly effective in painting clouds, but wet into wet expands this no-hard-edge softness to the whole composition. But, wait, there's more.

As the paper slowly dried, the edges began to hold and by the time I was ready to paint in the ponies, the paper was quite dry. When it became bone dry, I was able to do the exacting, calligraphic painting I wanted to do, such as sharpening on the ponies and branches in the trees.

IN GENERAL, wet into wet, because the paper is so charged with water, requires you to use less water in your brush than you would usually use and more pigment. Also, continuing to wet the paper, to keep it from drying too fast, is fraught with danger. If you add water with a clean brush to paper that is still damp, the result will be disaster, which is called *water edging*. What happens is that the new water floats some of the color that is already there, and the floating pigment gathers at the edge of the newly wet area and dries there, forming a harsh edge. And, once there, you cannot get rid of it. Don't do it.

On the other hand, when the paper has dried completely—bone dry, dust dry—you can do some correcting by taking a broad, clean brush, charging it with clear water, stroking it briskly over the area *just once,* and proceeding to repaint.

WET INTO WET is not easy. It takes practice, and, one hopes, with practice, increased skill. Once in graduate school I was made to repaint a wet into wet watercolor eight times before it was deemed acceptable.

Good luck, and don't become discouraged.

Trussum Pond, Delaware : Trees

Studying, sketching, and painting different types of trees.
How to treat trees in the foreground and middle ground
and those in the distance.

East of Laurel, Delaware, off Delaware Route 24, lies Trussum Pond, a picturesque pond with bald cypress trees, pines, and brown, cypress-stained water. Fishermen, trying their luck for perch, and canoeists seeking a calm, out-of-the-way body of water frequent the pond, as do occasional photographers and artists. I like to paint here because of the striking contrast between the trees and pond and the sunlight, as it cascades and filters through the leaves and is reflected in the surface of the water. There is often a yellowish film or scum on the edges of the pond and an abundance of lily pads. It is all very serene and visually striking.

Trussum Pond is only a mile or so beyond Trap Pond, which is well

marked, a popular (and usually well-populated) state park, where you will find picnicking, swimming, boating, fishing, hiking, and all sorts of recreational activities. It is here that families gather to enjoy the outdoors in a beautiful setting and in a variety of ways. Trap Pond, too, includes a vast bald cypress swamp area, but the whole ambiance is not nearly as tranquil as Trussum, its undeveloped neighbor.

THERE ARE some things to think about as you set out to paint trees. You cannot view a landscape, panoramic or otherwise, without seeing trees, sometimes acres and acres of them. Woods present problems different from those presented by a lone tree in the middle of a grassy field. In masses of trees, you are confronted with a vast array of greens and a variety of textures and light that affect the shading. To begin to understand the techniques of painting trees, though, we had best begin with the lone tree in a meadow—a maple tree, for example.

Choose one of two brushes. Select either a half-inch single-stroke flat or a round number 7. The half-inch flat turned on its side, with just a little water and color, dragged across the paper in short strokes creates the look of leaves (see color plate 15, fig. 1). A round brush used with a dabbing stroke will create a single leaf or group of leaves, depending on the amount of pressure placed on the brush (pl. 15, fig. 2).

The first thing to remember is that a tree trunk stands in the center of the tree. To portray this, paint the leaves first and then paint the trunk up through the middle of the leaves. There is a light and dark pattern to leaves that characterizes the tree as a whole (pl. 15, fig. 3). Paint the light leaves first—those that the sun shines on—then darken your color using blue, brown, or black and paint those leaves that are in shadow. Remember that the local color of the tree will vary with the type of tree you are painting and, naturally, with the season of the year. In the fall you have many options indeed. Once the leaves have been painted, the tree trunk is painted up through the center of the tree. Where the leaves are darkest is where you are most apt to see the trunk, since the darker leaves tend to be found in the center of the tree, in the shadow of the brighter leaves. Often there are openings among the leaves, and branches are seen silhouetted against the sky beyond. When you have rendered the tree cor-

Plate 15. Trees, *9" × 12"*

FIG. 1

FIG. 2

SUN
LEAF   LEAF IN
SHADOW

FIG. 3

FIG. 4

FIG. 5

FIG. 6

DISTANT TREES

rectly, you will finish up with a beautiful, three-dimensional tree (pl. 15, fig. 4).

Different kinds of trees look quite different from each other, but whatever their other distinctions, they are all three dimensional and will always need to be rendered with lights and darks to portray their individual character—not only their size, but their volume and the specific shape that reveals their species. Oaks, with their gnarled branches, for example, or willows, with their weeping boughs, present different challenges to the painter. Evergreens are, of course, quite different again. (It is best to paint them, by the way, as they grow—with short upward or downward diagonal strokes, using the local color.)

Trees in the middle ground blend together to form a distinct pattern of light and dark with varying color. They may be painted while the paper is damp (pl. 15, fig. 5) or with the paper dry (pl. 15, fig. 6). On the other hand, really distant woods—a long ways away—usually appear simply as a shape, similar to ground rows in stage scenery. These shapes on the horizon are usually seen as flat tones of blue, brown, or dull green, rather than having the patterns of light and dark that we have just described for trees in the middle ground. Paint the distant trees with the shape and color that you see.

BACK TO TRUSSUM POND. Having chosen my spot and set up my tripod and paint box, I began with a Winsor & Newton hot press block. The only drawing I did was to sketch in lightly the placement of the tree trunks. I then chose a number 8 round brush. The foliage was painted first, using sap green as my dominant, or local, color (see color plate 16). To the sap green I added yellows for the greens in the foreground and those leaves touched by sunlight. Touches of blues, browns, and black were added to the green for trees in shadow and for the deep blue-green of the pines. In this scene the foreground is in shadow and the distant

Plate 16. Trussum Pond, *12" × 16"*

trees are in sunlight. Because the scene is composed of a variety of shades of green, I found myself mixing a touch of this and a drop of that to my local color to attain the different shades. You will notice that there are a lot of different greens. The number 8 round allowed me to dab the paint for individual leaves and to spot the pine cones, as well as to strike in the tree trunks.

The small, blooming red flowers on the left of the composition furnish a nice contrast to the abundance of green. For the pond water I used a half-inch single-stroke flat brush, held horizontally. The horizontal strokes keep the water flat. Because I had no sketched lines to guide me, I looked very closely at the patterns of water and pond film and rendered the water only in and around the film. For the water I used cerulean blue, Payne's gray, and a touch of ivory black. After the water was dry—the painted water, of course—I painted the pond scum, briskly, with a yellow-green. When the whole surface was dry, I painted in the reflections from the trees. As soon as the foreground was again dry, I painted the cast shadow on the water with a wash of neutral tint.

CHAPTER TWELVE

Lewes, Delaware : Reflections

Observing and painting reflections on calm and rippled water.

Where the Delaware Bay joins the Atlantic Ocean, near Cape Henlopen, is the small town of Lewes, Delaware. Founded in 1631, it is the first town in the First State. Lewes (pronounced as if it were spelled Lewis) was settled by the Dutch and retains more than a touch of its seafaring past. The architecture of many of the homes reflects the town's history. A canal passes from Delaware Bay through Lewes and runs southeast to Rehoboth Beach, Rehoboth Bay, and the Indian River Inlet. In the past few years, Lewes has undergone a revitalization. The run-down piers and neglected buildings have been replaced by carefully restored structures, new condos, attractive shops, and trendy restaurants, particularly in the part of town near the picturesque canal. Front Street and the drive out Pilot Town Road are attractive, leading you to the end of the canal and Roosevelt Inlet. Every summer for these past thirty years, I have set up my painting box and rendered scenes along this heavily traveled waterway. The oldest marine railway in Lewes, with its Quonset hut, is one of my favorite spots. As on most marine railways, boats in varying degrees of disrepair sit up on chocks, waiting their turn for reconditioning, a new paint job, or whatever. Nearby, on the west end of town, Lewes has retained an old Life Saving Station and, next to it, a large, red light ship. These are favorite, not to say irresistible, painting subjects. They are frequently included in the workshops sponsored by the nearby Rehoboth Beach Art League. Chapter 8, on texture, includes a picture of the Life Saving Station recently painted as a demonstration for one of these workshops.

THE LEWES CANAL offers locations on both sides of the canal where reflections are a part of almost any painting. Reflections are fascinating. The reflections with which we're most familiar are those from a mirror, and thinking for a moment about images you see in a mirror will help you as you see reflections in water. If you look directly at a mirror on the wall—a vertical mirror—you will see yourself. Your own image bounces directly back from the reflective surface. Now visualize the mirror lying on the floor. As you look at it, you don't see yourself; rather, you see the "mirror image" of whatever is beyond it. In fact, you can see directly what is beyond the mirror and a reflection of it in the mirror at the same time. It is this phenomenon that is like reflections on water.

When water is calm and its surface is glassy smooth, it is a remarkably good mirror. If there is the slightest movement of the surface—caused by wind, for example—then the reflection is interrupted. A four-year-old

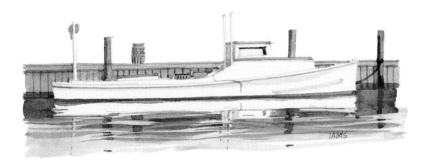

Plate 17. Reflections,
5" × 7" *each*

little boy once said, on seeing a choppy sea, "I don't want to go in the water; it has too many creases." It is these creases that disrupt smooth, mirrorlike reflections.

The closer you are to the water's surface, the longer (or deeper) a reflection of something on or above the water will be. The reflected image, from top to bottom, will be an elongated distortion of the original image. Ripples or any other slight movement on the surface of the water will often exaggerate this distortion, since part of the surface of each ripple or wave will be tilted closer to your angle of vision and the reflection will be made even longer. Broken water interrupts the reflection, making it appear to be in stripes. On the other hand, really rough water will provide little in the way of reflections. Sometimes there will be no reflection at all. You must look carefully and observe.

Color plate 17 provides two examples showing the influence of light on reflections. In the first example, the sun is shining on the hull, lighting it up, and the reflection is as bright a white as the hull itself. When the hull is in shadow, as in the second example, the reflection is dark, often darker than the color on the hull. In both instances, the reflections are not simple upside-down duplications of the workboat. The quiet movement of the water creates subtle crests and troughs of miniature waves, and only parts of each "wave" reflect the image back to the viewer. Again, you must look closely. Unfortunately, too many artists, not understanding reflections, leave them out altogether or overdo them. If you understand the basic principles, though, and really see what you look at, you will paint reflections effectively.

Like shadows, reflections should be kept transparent. If they are opaque, they resemble cut paper. Unlike shadows, however, which are always on the side opposite the light source, reflections always come directly toward you, regardless of where the light is coming from. As we see in the examples, the light on the hull affects the character of the reflection but not its position.

Lewes Reflections,
12" × 16"

I N L E W E S, to paint *Lewes Reflections* I returned to the marine railway, the one with the Quonset hut. The motor cruiser in the foreground was unexpected; usually there is a cruising sloop tied up in the first slip. After sketching the scene, I started with the sky and then, using cerulean blue and burnt sienna, painted the view of the opposite side of the canal. By using blue, I in effect put the buildings at a distance, making them recede into the background. Restaurants and boat slips line the north shore, and I simplified the buildings, but I made sure that the large restaurant on the right is recognizable by its silhouette. It is a well-known building and helps identify the scene. Painting the fishing boats next, I used cerulean blue and a little ivory black for the shaded side of the boat in the foreground. Much of the background is just suggested, and I took liberties with the many spars and telephone poles, placing them where I felt they were needed, except on the sailboats, where the masts and boom could not be altered. The pilings and bulkhead were painted next: burnt sienna and sepia for the shadowed side, yellow ochre for the sunny side. A little cobalt blue helped with the lighter wood and cast shadows. For the water I painted a light wash, using cerulean blue and ivory black, over the entire area. When it was dry, I used a mixture of Prussian blue and burnt sienna for the reflection from the boat and bulkhead. The reflection of the boat is quite dark because the hull is in shadow. A lighter version of the same color was used for the ripples that curve into the composition from left to right. Finishing touches included such details as the mooring lines and foreground grass. A touch of opaque white was added to reflect the white flying bridge on the motorboat.

The reflections from the larger pilings, as with all reflections, drop straight down and right at you. They are seen only on far sides of the waves or ripples in the water. From your vantage point, the near sides of ripples will reflect the sky but are at the wrong angle to form a mirror of what is beyond.

Reflections add immeasurably to scenes like this and are well worth the time you spend observing and studying in order to render them accurately.

CHAPTER THIRTEEN

Cape Henlopen State Park, Delaware :
Skies, Waves, and Dunes

Sketching and painting skies, surf, sand, and incidental figures.

Cape Henlopen State Park lies at the mouth of Delaware Bay, two miles east of Lewes, Delaware. During World War II, gun emplacements were erected there to defend the entrance to Delaware Bay, and although the guns are long gone, several observation towers remain, along with a few bunkers. The park also overlooks two breakwater lighthouses at the entrance of the bay, a round, brown one on the inner breakwater and a white, round light standing on the outer one. From Cape Henlopen, several times each day, you can watch the ferry that runs between Lewes and Cape May, New Jersey (the north cape of Delaware Bay). Ships flying foreign flags sail in and out of the bay, while some remain anchored awaiting their turn to proceed to Wilmington or Philadelphia.

The acres of dunes, dotted with pines and beach grasses, provide countless compositions suitable for painting. Once in the park, drive past the swimming facility to the end of the road. A tower on the left houses observers who report on incoming and outgoing ships. Just beyond the tower is one of several parking areas. From here, you have a beautiful panorama of the Atlantic Ocean and Delaware Bay. A short walk along the trail leads you to the beach and the ocean beyond. A bird sanctuary dominates the very tip of the park, but there are painting opportunities all around you.

The surf along the beach constantly changes. In general, I find that if the surf is good for swimming, it is not good for sketching or painting, but to each his own. As you set about painting the surf, though, you again must do a great deal of looking and watching and studying. This concentration will pay off. You will notice that, just as the wave curls, ready to break, the water turns a translucent green and then it crashes, with spray, onto the water rushing beneath it in the opposite direction. This backwash contains foam, sand, and reflections from the sky. What you see are myriad shades of blue, green, and a variety of sand colors. In a matter of seconds, a new wave approaches, and the ocean comes pounding down onto the sand again. And again. No two alike. Capturing this is a real challenge. A camera will help, since a photograph will arrest the image and give you a chance to study it in detail, but photographs can't really describe the ocean. Looking and sketching, looking and sketching, over and over again, is the only way to meet this challenge.

I USE THE TERM *incidental figures* to mean subordinate or casual figures introduced into a painting, whether or not a person was actually part of the original scene. In many instances, a person or a group of people placed in a composition will help the viewer relate to the painting. In other cases, the addition of a figure will help give a sense of scale to the work. Oriental painters, for example, to stress the beauty of the landscape, add small subordinate figures to make the mountains and trees more prominent. Architects use figures to establish proportions between humans and their surroundings.

Figures are not needed in all compositions. A landscape void of figures tends to suggest solitude and perhaps even a scene where no man

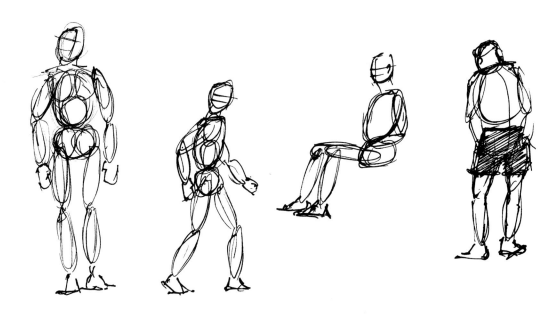

has been. The choice of using a figure or figures in a painting is up to the artist.

Not only here, but all down the Delmarva Peninsula, there are spectacular beaches. South from Henlopen are Rehoboth Beach, Dewey Beach, Bethany Beach, and Fenwick Island in Delaware; Ocean City and Assateague in Maryland; and more of Assateague plus Chincoteague in Virginia. There are, in short, miles of clean, broad beaches, with the ever-changing ocean on one side and dunes on the other. Once on the beach, you can often be out of sight of any manmade structure and sometimes very much alone. But there are also life-guarded bathing beaches in the communities I mentioned, dotted along the coast. At these, I often sit and sketch the people enjoying the sun and surf.

Bathers are usually on the move, so you must sketch quickly, much the way you study and sketch birds in flight. Look closely, then close your eyes, picture in your mind what you have seen, and then sketch. My sketches here show the ovals and "sausages" I use to set up the proportions of the human figure. There are other ways of reaching the proportions, but the ovals work well for me. Using the head as a unit of measure, I draw the figure about seven and a half heads tall, two heads wide at the chest and hip. Each person is different, however, so use your eye, and draw what you see.

In my studio, I often use a small mannequin that I pose and sketch. I sometimes use photographs (as in the case of the waterman in Saxis) and even have had myself photographed, in costume, to get a particular pose I wanted.

View from Cape Henlopen (color plate 18) is actually a composite. I took the artist's prerogative and rearranged the scene. Near the tip of Cape Henlopen State Park, I sketched the various elements I saw but placed them in different positions, creating my own composition. I did this on

Saxis Waterman,
6" × 10"

Plate 18. View from
Cape Henlopen,
14″ × 20″

14″ × 20″ Arches 140-pound hot press paper. I began, as I almost always do, with the sky, painting from the horizon up.

Although I have described in several earlier chapters the technique I use for painting skies, it is worth reviewing for two reasons. first, the sky should be painted first. Second, and more important, the sky establishes the mood and setting for the entire watercolor painting. It establishes not only the time of day, but also what kind of day it is: bright, crisp, and clear; overcast, eliminating dramatic shadows; foggy, perhaps, or threatening. Pay close attention to your skies. They are extremely important. They evoke an immediate response, and it is up to you to guide that response to your painting. Remember that you never get a second chance to make a first impression.

So, back to the painting. I first wet the entire sky area and then, with a one-inch single-stroke flat, using Payne's gray and a little cerulean blue, I started painting. Moving up, I added a little more Payne's gray and a touch of black. To this same mix, though made a little stronger, I added a touch of neutral tint. I then introduced patches of blue using cerulean blue. Notice that the strokes are predominately horizontal.

Having laid in the sky, I turned to the water. I used cerulean blue and ivory black, allowing the white of the paper to show at strategic places to indicate whitecaps and surf. The pine trees on the left are basically sap green and Prussian blue, with an occasional touch of sepia for the dead wood. For the sand color I used a very, very light neutral tint and burnt sienna. The beach grasses are sap green and gamboge in various proportions, though cadmium yellow deep, with Prussian blue, also works for some of the richer greens in the grass. By pinching the bristles on a flat brush, or even a round one, you can spread the bristles, giving them a whisker effect, which is an effective tool. By doing this and using upward strokes, you can create very realistic clumps of grass. For the taller clumps, I used a sharp-tipped round brush.

The figure is from one of my bathing-beach sketches. I used opaque white for this fellow's shirt. On a whim, I added the anchored ship for him to be looking at.

CHAPTER FOURTEEN

New Castle, Delaware :
Architectural Painting

*Sketching and painting bricks, windows, shutters, and
other details of buildings.*

Although many of the paintings accompanying earlier chapters include buildings, none has been devoted specifically to the various
requirements of a painting that is essentially architectural. Such paintings permit less latitude, less artistic license, than do most landscapes or
seascapes, and this chapter focuses on details that will need your close attention as you paint buildings as such.

First, drawing is all-important in an architectural painting. Correct
perspective is essential, but so also is attention to such things as the texture of building materials, window structure and placement, rooflines
and eaves and chimneys, steps and doorways, and so forth. In the end,

however, if a finished architectural painting presents a problem, if it simply is not a good painting, the chances are that at the root of the problem is poor draftsmanship.

To demonstrate architectural painting, I traveled to New Castle, Delaware, a beautiful town situated only a few miles southeast of Wilmington on the shore of the Delaware River. New Castle was settled in the middle of the seventeenth century as a Dutch fort. Ultimately, it became the seat of regional government, then the capital of the colony, and later, though very briefly, the capital of the State of Delaware. It was a bustling port and enjoyed unusual prosperity. In the early nineteenth century, however, with the opening of the Chesapeake and Delaware Canal to its south and later the railroad from Philadelphia to Baltimore through Wilmington, bypassing the town, New Castle lost its preeminence as a trading center and fell into a long, gradual decline. Although that was a difficult period for those who had to endure it, by having fallen into a slump the community retained, with little change resulting from "progress," its eighteenth-century character. As a result, the original section of town, surrounding the courthouse square, has cobblestone streets lined with stately trees and scores of lovely Colonial and Federal houses, meticulously maintained, often with gardens behind them, their facades rising directly from the edges of the brick sidewalks. To visit New Castle is to step back in time. Needless to say, you have many historic buildings to choose from as you set out to try your hand at architectural painting.

MY CHOICE for a painting was the George Read House, on the Strand (see color plate 19). This spectacular structure was built in 1801 and, with its twenty-two rooms, was the largest house in Delaware at the time. It has been fully restored and is now open as a museum. Its gardens, dating from 1847, are the oldest surviving gardens in the state.

I made several thumbnail sketches and took several photographs. The

Plate 19. The George
Read House,
14" × 19"

painting was made in my studio. I took my time completing the drawing.
As you will recall from chapter 2, on perspective, I prefer to relate the
lines and angles to each other rather than to construct (or imagine) vanishing points. Another technique that many artists use, especially when
a sketch is smaller than the painting is to be, is to draw a grid over the
sketch and a larger grid, very lightly, of course, on the watercolor paper.
By copying each square of the sketch into the corresponding larger
square on your paper, you retain the proportions of the original. This requires precision and, for me, is not worth the time it takes. But others
find it helpful, and you might want to try it.

My paper was 14" × 20" Lana 140-pound cold press. First, of course,
I painted the sky and then the trees on the left, introducing some fall colors for contrast.

As for the house, I used cadmium red, cadmium yellow, and a touch
of alizarin crimson, diluted, for the sunny side, painted with a half-inch
single-stroke brush and a quarter-inch flat. This combination worked

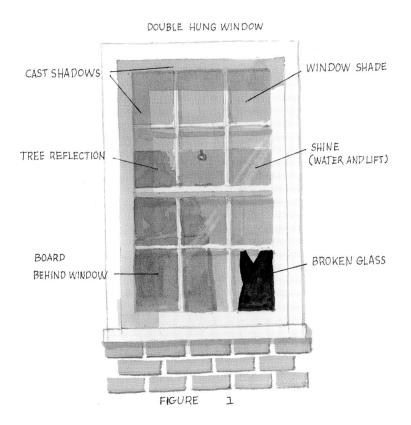

Plate 20. Window Panes, 8" × 10"

DOUBLE HUNG WINDOW

CAST SHADOWS

WINDOW SHADE

TREE REFLECTION

SHINE
(WATER AND LIFT)

BOARD
BEHIND WINDOW

BROKEN GLASS

FIGURE 1

very well. The house is constructed of brick, but from this distance color alone is sufficient to indicate that. Were I closer to the building, I would have to show individual bricks, at least in the sunlit areas, if not everywhere. Sunlight brings out the texture of a surface. The shadowed facade of the house was painted next, using the same colors but with a touch of ivory black added and less water. Next, the windows. To keep the windows from looking like postage stamps—something just pasted on—look closely. Look for details that alter or influence the look of the glass.

Drapes, curtains, shades, and an occasional internal detail will affect the otherwise flat appearance. I counted the panes and studied the woodwork (see color plate 20). I painted the panes of glass first. If there is no reflection in the glass, the panes will usually appear dark or black. On the shaded side of the building, the sky was reflected in the windows, so I painted the panes a cerulean blue, making sure to leave the woodwork white. The curtains behind the glass are indicated by darkening the area between the curtains. When these areas were dry, I painted the cast shadow on the windows. The window shades were drawn down on the sunny side of the first floor of the house, and for this I used a light yellow ochre for the panes.

Next I concentrated on the overhang of the roof and the intricate woodwork under the eaves. Then the spouts, gutters, and shutters. The dormers were the next challenge. Perspective is very important here, since the dormers protrude from the slanted surface of the pitched roof. In this instance, they line up vertically with the windows of the lower floors. The beautiful door and the window above it, because they are so distinctive, required particular attention to detail. Once these were accommodated, I turned to the steps and the plantings around the house and behind the wall.

Making sure the surface is dry and with a mix of the brick color darkened with ivory black, I stroked in the cast shadows. I was careful not to go over any area more than once. If the shadow dries too light, I let the paint dry and stroke it again. Remember, the surface must be bone dry before you apply a glaze, and you must apply it briskly, with assurance. Do not scrub.

The brick wall, the sidewalk, and the foreground were next. The figure and the car added to the sense of scale, and I finished off with the cast shadow falling in from the left.

A Painting Painted

have taken you on a painting tour of the Delmarva Peninsula, shar-
ing many of my favorite haunts. I have also shared, mostly by example, my passion to paint—and especially my enjoyment of painting outside, on location.

Being outdoors on a warm, sunny morning, with the sun casting long,
cool shadows across the terrain, offers a kind of stimulation impossible
to recreate within the four walls of a studio. The smell of sawdust and
varnish at the Cutts & Case boatyard in Oxford, the honking of a skein
of Canada geese lifting off a tidal pool at Blackwater National Wildlife
Refuge—these aromas and haunting sounds are found only out of doors.

Your senses will be sharpened as you look across the brown, cypress-stained water of Trussum Pond or as you respond to the rhythm of the chug, chug, chug of the one-lung gas engine on an Eastern Shoreman's skiff as he works his trotline on the Choptank near Tilghman Island. In short, I hope that you have found on this adventure, as I have, that painting on location is extremely exciting. It is as exciting for one who has been painting for several years as it is for a beginner.

I also hope you have found that not only do time and tide not wait, but neither does the sun linger, and light changes constantly. This makes it imperative to sketch and paint with decisiveness. You must attack your paper or canvas. Well, perhaps *attack* is too strong a word; *approach vigorously* might be better. Whatever the term, address the painting with the resolve to render it within a few hours. Nail it down. You will love the feeling of accomplishment as you complete a fine work of art painted on location. It is an enormously satisfying feeling—a richly rewarding experience indeed.

The Delmarva Peninsula contains a veritable cornucopia of locations to paint. I have led you to just a few, and you have doubtless discovered others. There are so many of them out there. Wherever you go, I hope you will nurture the passion to paint—the passion that I have found an irrepressible part of my being and that makes every painting a fresh, new, exhilarating challenge, waiting to be met. I hope the same for you.

Good luck.

Library of Congress Cataloging-in-Publication Data

Iams, James Drake, 1927–
     Painting the Eastern Shore : a guide to Chesapeake
and Delaware places and how to capture them in watercolors / James Drake Iams.
          p.   cm
     ISBN 0-8018-6232-9 (alk. paper)
     1. Eastern Shore (Md. and Va.)—In art.   2. Watercolor
painting—Technique.   I. Title.
ND2365.I24   1999
751.42'243'097521—DC21   99-19001